PRAISE FOR
INTIMACY WITH GOD

"Randy Clark has been a kind and generous friend for decades, suffering and celebrating with us in some of the most difficult mission fields on the planet. We have always appreciated his unfailing curiosity about our shared faith in a world of trials, mysteries, and miracles—but above all we have enjoyed his childlike enthusiasm for the gospel, for which we, too, have been so glad to give our lives."

—HEIDI G. BAKER, PhD, COFOUNDER AND EXECUTIVE
CHAIRMAN OF THE BOARD, IRIS GLOBAL

"Randy shares from his years of experience and faithfulness, teaching each of us to step into deeper intimacy with Jesus in order that we may all fulfill the greatest commandment to love and to bring a display of God's miraculous power, truly living as the disciples of Jesus. Randy's childlike faith, humility, and deep understanding of Scripture will bless you as you delve into this book."

—JOHN AND CAROL ARNOTT, CATCH THE FIRE

"Intimacy with God is our greatest calling and the ultimate achievement in life. I pray this book ignites a flame deep within your soul to know Jesus, the lover of our souls."

—MICHAEL KOULIANOS, FOUNDER, JESUS IMAGE

"It's my privilege to endorse this book by my friend Randy Clark. Our ministry isn't meant to be something we do in our own power; it flows from intimacy with God. As I read this book, it encouraged me personally to trust the Lord more deeply in His leading and for His miracles."

—CRAIG KEENER, F.M. AND ADA THOMPSON PROFESSOR OF
BIBLICAL STUDI   Y

"This book powerfully inspires readers to seek to know God in richer and more glorious ways."

—KATHERINE RUONALA, SENIOR LEADER OF GLORY CITY CHURCH, BRISBANE, AUSTRALIA; FOUNDER AND FACILITATOR, THE AUSTRALIAN PROPHETIC COUNCIL; AUTHOR, *SUPERNATURAL FREEDOM*

"Drawn from years of theological study and witnessing incredible supernatural events around the world, *Intimacy with God* teaches us how friendship with God is the wellspring of all transformation, personally and globally. I encourage you to read this book with an open heart and an open mind."

—REV. SAMUEL RODRIGUEZ, PRESIDENT, NATIONAL HISPANIC CHRISTIAN LEADERSHIP CONFERENCE; AUTHOR, *SURVIVE TO THRIVE*

"I was challenged and stirred by [this book's] unique revelation and stories . . . I highly recommend this soon to be a classic book by one of the greatest followers of Christ and modern-day revivalists that I know. Do yourself a favor and get this explosive read right away."

—SEAN SMITH, AUTHOR, *PROPHETIC EVANGELISM*

"The outpouring of the Holy Spirit is not only to restore us to intimate relationship with God but also to restore our ability to hear His voice and to give us the power to obey His Word. Intimacy should lead us beyond the prayer closet into the streets to do the miraculous for His glory!"

—KIM MAAS, FOUNDER, KIM MAAS MINISTRIES; INTERNATIONAL SPEAKER; AUTHOR, *PROPHETIC COMMUNITY*

"Staying consistent with revealed scriptural truth and evidence from eye-witnesses, we are shown the pathway to enrich our own spiritual lives and help others experience the fullness of the gospel of the kingdom."

—PHILL OLSON, DIRECTOR OF PRODUCT SALES AND DEVELOPMENT, GLOBAL AWAKENING BOOKSTORE

INTIMACY
with GOD

CULTIVATING A LIFE OF DEEP FRIENDSHIP
THROUGH OBEDIENCE

RANDY CLARK

EMANATE
BOOKS

Intimacy with God

© 2021 Randy Clark

Published in Nashville, Tennessee, by Emanate Books, an imprint of Thomas Nelson. Emanate Books and Thomas Nelson are registered trademarks of HarperCollins Christian Publishing, Inc.

ISBN 978-0-7852-2434-1 (eBook)
ISBN 978-0-7852-2433-4 (TP)

Library of Congress Cataloging-in-Publication Data

Names: Clark, Randy, 1952- author.
Title: Intimacy with God : cultivating a life of deep friendship through obedience / Randy Clark.
Description: Nashville, Tennessee : Emanate Books, an imprint of Thomas Nelson, [2021] | Includes bibliographical references. | Summary: "Randy Clark examines how Jesus and the Scriptures (focusing on the book of John) demonstrate the vital relationship between intimacy, obedience, and the miraculous as a blueprint for all believers. Dr. Clark explores how these aspects of Jesus' relationship with the Father bring glory to God. Combining sound biblical teaching with keen insight, Dr. Clark invites us to go deeper by asking and studying the following questions"-- Provided by publisher.
Identifiers: LCCN 2021007002 (print) | LCCN 2021007003 (ebook) | ISBN 9780785224334 (paperback) | ISBN 9780785224341 (epub)
Subjects: LCSH: Bible. John--Criticism, interpretation, etc. | Spirituality--Christianity. | God (Christianity)--Worship and love. | Intimacy (Psychology)--Religious aspects--Christianity. | Friendship--Religious aspects--Christianity.
Classification: LCC BS2615.52 .C53 2021 (print) | LCC BS2615.52 (ebook) | DDC 226.5/06--dc23
LC record available at https://lccn.loc.gov/2021007002
LC ebook record available at https://lccn.loc.gov/2021007003

Printed in the United States of America

21 22 23 24 25 LSC 10 9 8 7 6 5 4 3 2 1

DEDICATION

First, I dedicate this book to my wife and daughter who have lived a life of intimacy with Jesus. My wife, DeAnne, is such an inspiration to me. Her prayers of intercession in times of crisis are answered so frequently, so quickly, it is amazing. I tell her she is God's pet. Our daughter, Johannah, was hearing from God when she was only three years of age and spoke words that were so important to her mother. Later, God was speaking to Johannah as a young teen before He spoke to me about moving our family halfway across America.

Second, I dedicate this book to the rest of my family: my three sons, Joshua, Josiah, and Jeremiah; my son-in-law, David; my daughters-in-law, Tonya, Allie, and Lizzie; and my grandchildren, Simeon, Selah, Malachi, Harper, Juliette, William, Nova, Ember, and Ronan.

Third, I dedicate this book to my spiritual children: associate ministers Charity, William, and Brian; the fifty-seven others who were interns or traveling partners with me over the past twenty-six years; and my students of the Global Awakening Theological Seminary, Global Awakening College of Ministry, and the Global School of Supernatural Ministry. I want to acknowledge the following students whose testimonies appear in this book: Brian, Kaise, Matt, Jessika, Caleb, David, Will, and Benjamin. I am proud of them for stepping out in faith to minister to others. Their stories are only a small sample of the many testimonies from students in the school's physical healing course. It is my hope that I have modeled before you a passion for the kingdom of God, love for the Savior, and compassion for people. I want to encourage all of you to be all you can be in His kingdom, to pursue intimacy, obedience, revelation, faith, and signs and wonders for His glory.

CONTENTS

FOREWORD

I AM THE LAST PERSON I WOULD HAVE EVER expected to be asked to write a foreword to Randy Clark's latest book. I am not a world-class evangelist, or a learned scholar, or a famed expert on the gifts of the Spirit as Randy is.

All I am is a seeker of *truth*. I have been so since I became a believer in Jesus, Yeshua, my Savior as a young twelve-year-old girl with big dreams sitting in a darkened movie theater in Annapolis, Maryland. I believe Almighty God—Divinity—meets all needy people like you and me—*humanity*—right where our hearts and our dreams live and breathe.

I had wanted to be an actress and a singer since I made my debut fresh from my mother's womb. The God who created me in that very womb and placed those very dreams inside my heart in that dark and secret and sacred place had a plan for me even then.

By the closing credits of the film I had watched, *The Restless Ones*, I had a choice to make: Would I follow the way of the world, or would I choose to follow The Way, Himself? I had grown up in a loving home with a Jewish father and a Gentile mother. We were not a religious, churchgoing family. But I was taught that God was real.

That evening so many years ago in that dilapidated little movie theater, still a child in many ways, I heard a voice. I knew it was Jesus. It wasn't audible but it cut to the very core of my soul as if it was a symphony.

"Kathie," He said, "I love you and if you'll trust Me, I'll make something beautiful out of your life."

I literally ran down that aisle to receive that promise and sign the covenant!

He who promised me has been faithful. I look back at that moment as the singular most significant decision I have ever made. I now have a lifetime of experience with this Savior/Friend/Redeemer/Lover of my soul. I can proclaim His glory to the nations and the heavens beyond because the God I was told was real has proven He *is* real every day of my existence.

I have seen miracles in other people's lives. I have experienced many miracles in my own.

I have encountered demons and I have watched them flee when they were commanded to leave in the name of Jesus.

The gifts of the Spirit described in the Bible (1 Corinthians 12:8–10) are every bit as alive and powerful today as they were in the days of Jesus. Jesus Himself promised in John 14:12: "Truly, truly I tell you, whoever believes in me will do the works I have been doing, and they will do even greater things than these, because I am going to the Father."

He sent His Holy Spirit to all who believe in Him that *we might continue His good work in us* to heal a hurting, rotting, broken, and hopeless world full of people who *need* Him. To deny that the gifts of the Spirit are still real and available today is to deny the very promise of the One we say we believe in.

And thus we choose a life in the shadows of the truth instead of the full light and radiance and power of the Son Himself.

"Fear not" is the most frequently mentioned commandment in all of Scripture.

Randy Clark is a man who has lived out his life of faith fearlessly and has passed on this living truth to anyone who had ears to hear . . . and hearts to believe.

I pray that as you read *Intimacy with God*, you, too, will lay down all fear and step out in faith, believing to walk on the water with Jesus.

You, too, will move mountains.

You, too, will do miracles.

For in the name of Jesus, you can do *All Things!*

Kathie Lee Gifford

INTRODUCTION

IT IS EXCITING TO REALIZE THAT GOD COMMUNI-
cates with us, especially when that communication takes you into
an experience of the power of God that touches the life of another
person in a profound and beneficial way. The person may benefit
in a number of different ways by the information God gives you
to share with them. Sometimes this information results in healing. This healing can be physical or emotional. It can come in the
form of deliverance from addictions or demons or both. God might
bring provision, either supernatural or natural, and reconciliation
between friends or family or with God. But how does this happen?
And what are some of the ways in which God communicates with
us? I see it happen through faith—faith created as God's Holy Spirit
conveys information to individuals who have learned how to recognize these communications as coming from God.

You may be asking, "So, how exactly does this kind of communication work?" We know that God communicates with us through
His Son, Jesus, and through His written living Word, the Bible. I
have often heard people say, "The words of Scripture seemed to
jump off the page." When God highlights a portion of Scripture
that He wants to use in the moment to bring our attention to a

specific need, or to give direction for a current situation, charismatics call it a "*rhema* word." A *rhema* word is a word from heaven, through an individual, about something they are to do, which carries with it the power of God to bring the word given into reality. *Rhema is* also often the means used by God to build or create a gift of faith or a major increase in faith for ministry related to the *rhema*. *Rhema* words do not contribute to new doctrine or Scripture, but to the issues of life where direction, help, or encouragement is needed. Similarly, God sometimes gives us words of knowledge, which are His instructions for what He wants to do. The gifts of words of knowledge or prophecy don't add any new truth to our faith but are ways God provides us with new information that encourages our faith. God also communicates through dreams, open visions, impressions, mental pictures, feeling pain that is not your pain, and even seeing words that supernaturally appear in your mind's eye. God often communicates through divine appointments that are not mere coincidences but are orchestrated by the Holy Spirit.

When I speak of communication through faith, I am referring to faith in two different ways. The first refers to the core beliefs we have about God, the Christian faith, and its doctrines, and it is related to truth—the truth made known to us in the Bible. The second refers to the faith to trust or believe so strongly that one actually acts on the first kind of faith. It is possible to obtain new information from God about practical, specific things in life, information He is giving to us for a purpose. This type of communication from God is not the same as the truth that comes from the Bible. No new truth can be added to our canon. This is an important distinction to keep in mind as you read this book and the testimonies I am going to share with you.

The Bible itself, however, presents narrative accounts of people who were receiving communication (revelation) that was true communication from God and true revelation, but the Bible did not include what the revelation was or what the words were. Other prophets and their ministries are mentioned, but the quality of the revelation, the nature of it, was not such that it merited being included in the canon. A concise way of saying this is that the Bible indicates there was *special* revelation that became part of the canon, and there was also *specific* revelation that was not deemed to be included in the canon.

These testimonies illustrate ordinary people receiving communication from God that He intends to use to touch lives profoundly and beneficially. They are drawn from the experiences of my interns and associates, students in my seminary class on physical healing, as well as lay people who work in diverse fields such as banking, marketing, farming, and in the home. Additionally, you will find testimonies from pastors, including mainline denomination pastors, itinerant pastors from around the world, and missionaries. For my seminary students, part of their coursework is to have at least one experience every week for six weeks where they receive a communication from God, either in the form of a word of knowledge or prophecy that provides opportunity for them to pray for someone in need of healing, deliverance, or salvation. The general age range of these students is early twenties through forties, although a few are older. Their testimonies give witness to how followers of Jesus today can live the intimate, supernatural life He intends for us to live in the power of His Spirit.

This book is not focused on theology alone or solely on discussing scriptural interpretations that are important but can be debated. It is my desire that you see and understand what God is doing in the world today. Many people find God's miracles hard to believe and therefore distrust what they are hearing. Jesus says that we are to judge the false prophets by their fruit. In other words, when you look at the results of the miraculous, do you see the fruit of God as found in Scripture or something else—the rotten fruit of the devil, or the ability of the human spirit and not the Holy Spirit of God? The testimonies you are about to read are stories of the fruit of God and clearly illustrate the fruit of communication from God to believers today. The testimonies from students in my seminary class are very recent—from the past six weeks as of this writing. (The students shared many more case studies than those I have used in the book; thirty students submitted 180 case studies.) As you read through these testimonies, I believe you will agree that they profoundly illustrate communications between the Good Shepherd and His sheep. Jesus said, "My sheep hear my voice" (John 10:27 ESV).

I want to begin with a testimony from Brian Starley, an associate minister on my staff. Brian went to the Global School of Supernatural Ministry for two years, after which he was invited to be my intern for a year.[1] He is in his midtwenties. I am amazed at the accuracy of the details Brian receives in words of knowledge—details such as names, addresses, and vocations. Brian is married to a brilliant young woman who is going to university while working for our ministry full time. The first time I read this testimony, I wept at the revelation of God's grace and love demonstrated in this encounter. His sheep truly do hear His voice.

Recently, I had the privilege of witnessing the life-changing power that accompanies a word of knowledge from God. This power not only changed the lives of the individuals I ministered to, but it affected me enormously as well. I was walking to the local grocery store, and as I approached it, I saw a group of men gathered outside. There were four of them, and they were all riding Harley Davidson motorcycles. Later I found out that they were members of a gang, but initially I was not aware of that fact. This particular word of knowledge had come to me in a dream the night before. In the dream I saw a picture of a large black leather jacket. On this leather jacket was the image of a harpy from Greek mythology, and the name Brandon was sown in red letters underneath the harpy. Next to the name Brandon was the word *cancer*, also in red. Honestly, I did not have a second thought about the dream, and it wasn't on my mind as I headed to the store. Upon getting closer, I saw that all the bikers had harpies sown onto their jackets. Immediately, I remembered the dream and knew that it had been God speaking to me and that I needed to act on what I had heard.

I felt quite a bit of fear as I approached the bikers. They were all huge guys and looked very rough. It was intimidating for me. However, I knew that I needed to be obedient to what the Lord had shown me in the dream. In Dr. Clark's teaching on the Gospel of John, he outlines the relationship between intimacy, revelation, and obedience, pointing out that we move in the miraculous realm from obedience, and that this obedience comes from the ability to hear God's voice. This hearing out of intimacy will thrust us into obedience. I have learned that in order to best steward what God has given me, obedience must come first, despite my feelings on the matter.

As I approached the men, they noticed me, and I could tell from their body language that they were not happy I was there. When I got closer one of the men snapped at me, "What do you want?"

I knew God had sent me, but I didn't know what to say to them. Remembering that I saw the name written beneath the harpy in my dream, I asked, "Which one of you is named Brandon?" Shocked, they looked at each other and then turned to the man on my right. He said, "Who's asking?"

I replied, "I know this will sound crazy, but I'm a Christian, and sometimes God speaks to me through dreams. Last night, I dreamed about the harpy on your jacket. Your name was also on the jacket, along with the word *cancer*."

From what I had seen in the dream, I thought that Brandon was the one who currently had cancer, but I soon found out that was not the case. Tears came to Brandon's eyes. I was floored by what he said next, and I am holding back tears now as I write this.

He told me, "God must have been the one to tell you that dream. I haven't talked to God in a long time, not since my mother passed away from cancer."

As Brandon began to cry, the others with him became emotional as well. He told me through tears how he was raised in a God-fearing home but abandoned it all after he lost his mother to breast cancer. He said that this led him to join the Warlocks Motorcycle Club, which all the men present were members of. The harpy is the emblem for the group.

As Brandon told me his story, I received a secondary word of knowledge that let me know how to pray. The Holy Spirit said, *Tell him that his mother is with Me [God], and I want to heal his heart as well as his degenerated disc.* I told Brandon what I had just heard, and he wept further as he said to me that his L-4 vertebra had significantly deteriorated from the impact of the various bikes he's ridden. Knowing that I needed to pray for both his physical and spiritual healing, I asked if I could place my hand on his shoulder and pray for him. He agreed and I decided to pray for Brandon's back first. I selected a prayer of command since I was aware of the cause of the injury and I knew it to be physical. Therefore, I needed to speak to his disc to be restored. I began by praying, "Holy Spirit, come and release healing to Brandon's back. I speak to his vertebra, and command it to be made whole in the name of Jesus."

As I prayed, I began to sense heat coming from Brandon's body. I asked if he could feel anything, and he confirmed that there was heat all over him but specifically in his lower back. I asked him to try and do something that he couldn't do before. I did this because we know that responding in an act of faith is essential, and we see a high percentage of people healed when they begin to move their bodies. As Brandon began to move and bend over, he said that his pain was much less than before. I asked him, "On a scale from one to ten, how much better would you say it is?" He said, "Usually the pain sits at around an eight to ten all the time. Before you prayed, it was an eight, and now I would say it's a three."

I asked to pray one more time, letting him know that sometimes we see people healed in progression. He agreed once more, and I prayed the same prayer as before. I asked that he examine his back a second time, and he excitedly proclaimed that it was completely pain free. I thanked God for what He had done and asked Brandon if he wanted to rededicate his life to Jesus. He had not stopped weeping throughout our entire interaction, and he continued to weep as he told me, "Yes!"

Before I could tell him to repeat after me, he was already repenting and telling Jesus that he wanted to serve Him, to return to the way his mother had raised him. It was evident that he was truly sincere in his prayer. The other bikers were so touched that they wanted to receive Jesus as well!

After Brandon finished praying, I prayed with the other men there who wanted to be born again. I explained the significance of this and briefly shared with them the importance of turning from sin. I encouraged them to begin reading the Bible and to go to church, and I shared that I knew of multiple biker churches that meet near them, since they might be more comfortable to start in that setting. I prayed once more for God to seal His work in them and thanked them for letting me pray with them. Before we parted, I encouraged them to share their experience with God with everyone they knew in the Warlocks club.

This was an amazing experience that I will never forget.

I was struck by Brian's willingness to step out in faith to obey God. Faith is spelled R-I-S-K. I hope as you continue to read you will develop both the faith and passion to enter into the supernatural lifestyle of colaboring with Jesus. What the apostle Paul wrote to the Colossian church is true for us—that the revelation of Christ in you is the hope of glory, and that we labor with all of His energy that works so mightily within us (Col. 1:27).

This book is written on the premise that miracles, healing, signs and wonders have not ceased, based upon the evidence of Scripture,[2] church history,[3] and the experience of the mission field since the beginning of the twentieth century and especially today.[4] Solid evidence from church history indicates that miracles, healings, and signs and wonders have continued and, in fact, have exploded in the twentieth and twenty-first centuries, not only in the majority of the world, where the church is growing the fastest, but also in the Western world. This continuity is the consistent message of John's gospel, with its focus on the importance of the miraculous and how intimacy with Father, Son, and Holy Spirit is tied to revelation, which is a major cause of the grace of faith. I call it "confident faith." This grace gift of faith is the impetus of healing, miracles, signs and wonders. Throughout the book we will be using contemporary stories from a seminary class I am currently teaching on physical healing. The focus of this book is the intimate, supernatural life of Jesus and what we can learn from it, particularly His signs and wonders, His healings, and His miracles.

Of the four gospels, none of them comes close to John's gospel in emphasizing the divinity of Jesus and focusing on the relationship between faith and the miraculous. Though Matthew, Mark, and Luke—the Synoptic Gospels—describe more miracles and more accounts of healings and deliverance than John, they do not connect faith in Jesus to the miracles as strongly as John does. Contrary to much of what I learned in college and seminary, John's gospel has a very favorable understanding of faith, connecting healings, miracles, and deliverances to faith in Jesus.

A second focus of this book is the signs recorded in John's gospel connected to obedience—hearing, seeing, and obeying what the Father was saying and doing, and the implications of this kind of obedience for Christians today. The theological issue related to this subject is *immediacy* (direct experience of the presence of God or communication with God—the communication of knowledge from God and God's gifts to enable us to act on His communication). These gifts are expressions of God's own energies within us by the Holy Spirit. In practical terms, immediacy raises the question, How are we as followers of Jesus to see and hear what the triune God—Father, Son, and Holy Spirit—is communicating to us? I believe the answer is, as the saying goes, "better caught than taught." Telling stories of how God uses people is very instructive, not so much with rational knowledge but with experiential knowledge. In fact, this is how Jesus discipled others. He did not use only one method of discipleship—teaching or demonstrating—but both teaching *and* demonstrating. That is why so much of this book consists of case studies from students in the physical healing class at Global Awakening Theological Seminary. I believe as you read their stories the curtain will be pulled back and that which had been hidden will be revealed.

A third focus of this book is the insights gained from the Upper Room Discourse between Jesus and His disciples, recorded in John 13:31 to 16:33, which is one of the deepest and most obvious portions of the Bible that reveal how Christians are meant to live the more abundant, victorious, supernatural lifestyle demonstrated by Jesus. This passage of Scripture gives the greatest and clearest insight into the issue of immediacy, with God coming, empowering, enlightening, and communicating directly to us, His followers, with no other mediating source or agency. Immediacy takes seriously the Bible's emphasis on God's people, His sheep, hearing His voice and responding. It values the *rhema* aspect of God's voice to His children, considering the Orthodox Church's understanding of God's gifts being expressions of God Himself that are related by His energies. Additionally, I'll draw parallels between Paul's references to *Christ in you, the hope of glory* and the insights of Jesus from the Upper Room Discourse pertaining to the Holy Spirit—the Helper, Advocate, Counselor, Comforter—the One called to our side to help in our time of need.

When we experience a gift of the Holy Spirit, we are actually experiencing more than a gift; we are experiencing the immediacy of God Himself. Receiving revelation from God implies immediacy. In other words, God has to make known what He wants us to do before we can do it. This is not subjectivity, not mysticism. It is a relational experience where we do not look inside to discover our truth but become aware of the Holy Other, who said, "I am the way and the truth and the life" (John 14:6)—the triune God who creates mysterious terror and awe, the Holy One of Israel who has given us our burning-bush moment.[5] Many of the prophets' calls begin with the experience of God bringing them visions, dreams, and hearing Him speak to them. Sometimes the experiences were in dreams. The evangelism of Europe rather than Asia was due to Paul's dream of the man from Macedonia calling him to come to Macedonia.

My own personal journey to arrive at confident faith and its relationship to healing, miracles, deliverances, signs, and wonders has been a long one. I majored, minored, and took all my electives in college in religious studies. My experience in both college and seminary was an introduction to a method of interpreting the Bible that was influenced by Western rationalism, rooted in a non-supernaturalistic worldview. The miracles of Scripture were either accounted for by natural explanations or seen as legends or myths—stories meant to teach theological truths but not rooted in actual history. Professors held a suspicious or critical view of anything supernatural in most of my religion courses, based on a liberalism that rejects the supernatural worldview or cessationism that some conservative professors hold to. Cessationists believe in the miraculous worldview of the Bible, yet maintain that gifts of healing, miracles, tongues, and interpretation of tongues ended with the death of the apostles or the canonization of the Bible. In this cessationist view, the miraculous ceased—therefore Christians should not expect it anymore. Later, I discovered that the historical method used by cessationists for the post-biblical period was the same as the historical method used by the liberals for the biblical period, which the conservatives rejected for the biblical period. Additionally, many commentators, especially Protestants, wrongly reinterpreted prophecy as preaching.

Christian rationalism denigrates faith related to or based upon the supernatural—the signs and wonders of the Bible—viewing it as *inferior* to faith not associated with signs and wonders. Those who hold this view use two passages in John's gospel as proof-texts for this negative view of faith related to signs and wonders: John 4:48 and John 20:29. This interpretation of John's view of the supernatural comes from a negative perspective and is actually the exact opposite of what the book of John states. Faith related to signs and wonders is not inferior in quality, which will be explained later in the book.

My faith was so weakened by my college experience, so undermined by my religious studies, that I was left with a great many unanswered questions. In the hope of putting my faith back together, I decided to go three more years to seminary to pursue a master of divinity degree. In seminary, I tried to find the more conservative professors and play the devil's advocate, with the hope that the conservative professors would have answers for me that would refute the liberal teachings I was struggling with. Some of my doubts were dealt with, but some of my courses with liberal professors raised other doubts. In my last year of study for the master's degree, I took a course titled Biblical Authority and the Modern Mind. The required reading for this course turned on a light bulb in my head that would reset my faith. One of the books we had to read was *The Historian and the Believer* by Van A. Harvey. The book was committed to a very liberal view of the Bible and to the higher-critical method of interpreting the Bible, including the rejection of the supernatural.

While reading about the underlying philosophical view that supports the higher-critical method, I suddenly realized that for almost seven years I had been taught a method of interpreting the Bible that was based upon an antisupernatural worldview. I disagreed with this antisupernatural worldview primarily because I had personally received significant healing from life-threatening conditions just before being called into the ministry at the age of eighteen. As a result of my experience, healing had become the anchor of my faith in the continuation of God's ability to work miracles in the Bible and throughout church history, even in 1977, when this realization came to me. Years later, I found myself returning to seminary at fifty-nine years of age for a doctoral degree. I would pursue that degree while traveling 245 to 265 days a year. While writing my doctoral thesis, *A Study of the Effects of Christian Prayer on Pain or Mobility Restrictions from Surgeries Involving Implanted Materials*, I discovered a negative interpretation of the passages in John's gospel on the relationship between faith and the supernatural, signs and wonders, and healings and miracles. This interpretation was not from my professors at the seminary, but from the research I was doing for my thesis, and it revealed the hostility of many biblical commentators and interpreters toward signs and wonders.

Between the time I graduated from seminary in 1977 and the time I returned to seminary in 2011, I experienced a radical change in my life. Vestiges of my liberal theology of doubt and suspicion of the supernatural, including doubts regarding angels and demons, were exorcised from my worldview. This came about after I was filled with the Holy Spirit, received prophecies from pastor John Wimber in January 1984, and attended a healing seminar held in my Baptist church in March 1984. During the three days of the seminar, I saw more than fifty healings take place, including the instant healing of my wife's severe TMJ. These experiences launched me into a life filled with the exciting pursuit of the presence and power of God through the preaching of the gospel, with an expectation of signs and wonders following the preaching. I wasn't following signs and wonders. I was following Jesus' Great Commission with the expectation that signs and wonders would follow, and they did. The gospel, with signs following, points to Jesus and causes His name to be exalted as it was in Ephesus (Acts 19).

During the forty-four years between 1977 and 2021, I have had the privilege of seeing the blind see, the deaf hear, the lame walk, and the dying restored to life. I have had the joy of seeing multiple sclerosis, Parkinson's disease, ALS, mental illness (including paranoid schizophrenia), and cancer healed. I saw three women healed: one woman was facing the amputation of her foot after fifteen years of walking on crutches, another an amputation near the hip because of a cancerous tumor in her femur, and the third was facing amputation below the knee. Then I began to see people healed who were in chronic pain or had lost range of motion from surgeries that involved implanting metal. Many received healing instantly. Their pain would disappear or lessen by at least 80 percent, with movement restored by at least 80 percent, and for many it was 100 percent. In the course of research for my thesis, I pored over a wealth of medical publications regarding pain, especially pain due to failed back surgery. I discovered that the medical community considered even 20 percent improvement of pain from failed back surgery to be a great improvement. Yet I was only including in my study those who experienced 80 percent or more improvement and were still seeing impressive results.[6]

What made me want to go back to seminary at fifty-nine years of age? While teaching on healing, I was recruited by the leading professor of theology at that seminary. He urged me to consider a doctorate. As I did, I clearly saw the need for me to get an advanced degree on the topic of the miraculous. A doctorate would afford me the academic credibility needed to address the pressing need, in both charismatic and evangelical circles, for better theology regarding healing. Too many weird practices and beliefs were beginning to be preached. Hyper-grace (an emphasis upon not needing to confess sins to God or ask for forgiveness: to overemphasize grace related to justification and to underemphasize grace for sanctification—or even totally devalue sanctification) and universalism were beginning to be accepted. Liberal and cessationist beliefs needed to be addressed, as both were having an impact on the church, resulting in a poor model of discipleship with no emphasis upon what Jesus modeled, taught, and commissioned the church to do: to heal the sick, cast out demons, and bring good news to the poor (Matt. 10:8).

I was allowed to take on two professors of my choice and establish the Randy Clark scholars program at the seminary. These two professors would oversee two groups formed with a focus on creating a strong biblical theology that would be the foundation upon which the practices of the gifts of the Spirit could be built. I wanted to create apologists for third-wave theology, which was part of the signs and wonders movement, and scholars who believed that all the gifts continued in the history of the church and are in fact continuing in this time. I call this the *continuationist* position, with theology based upon the insights of the Baptist scholar at Fuller Theological Seminary, Dr. George Eldon Ladd, in his "now and not yet" emphasis of the kingdom. Today, I am the president of Global Awakening Theological Seminary and one of its adjunct professors. Ours is a seminary that wants to be known for its commitment to both the Word of God and the Spirit of God, to be a continuationist school committed to kingdom theology of the "now and not yet." We want to be a place to learn how to interpret the Word of God and be challenged to move in the Spirit of God. A place where you learn how to exegete, not eisegete, the Scripture. (To *exegete* a passage is to draw from the passage its author's intended meaning. To *eisegete* a passage is to read into it your view, which is not the intended meaning of the original author. To exegete is good and to eisegete is negative.) A place where you learn how to expulse evil spirits from people; a place to learn how to work with the Spirit of God to heal the sick and diseased; a place to learn about God's heart for the brokenhearted, the captives, the oppressed, and the poor. In short, a place where people learn how to live out the gospel in the power of the Spirit in the world today.

Out of my ten years of theological and biblical studies, my favorite professor was Dr. Jon Ruthven. His book *On the Cessation of the Charismata: The Protestant Polemic on Post-biblical Miracles* was one of my favorite books during my studies. I am grateful for Dr. Ruthven's influence on my life. Here is the "Implications and Conclusion" to his book, which is quite pertinent to this book.

The frequent failure to respond to God's commands to manifest the Kingdom of God in power is fully shared by most believers, "charismatics" and non-charismatics alike. Both groups shape their theology and consequent practice on the basis of their own experience—or lack of it—rather than on a fresh and radical (in its original sense) view of Scripture. The presence or absence of certain charismata in one's experience proves nothing at all about one's spiritual status or destiny (Matt. 7:21–22). Neither group (charismatics or non-charismatics) is more or less "saved" than the other; both are at once sinful, but justified by grace alone. Nevertheless, the New Testament offers patterns as to how the gospel is to be presented, received, and lived out. We must not attempt to reframe our failures into virtues, that is, by allowing what the New Testament describes as "unbelief" in and for the gifts of God, to be construed as having chosen "the better way" of a "stronger faith" without them. The rabbis' intellectualized biblical knowledge, which led to their cessationism, prompted Jesus to affirm that they knew (in the biblical sense) "neither the Scriptures nor the power of God" (Matt. 22:29, Mark 12:24).

Much divisiveness over the gifts of the Spirit today derives from a premise common to both sides of the debate: evidentialism. If spiritual gifts are adduced as proofs of spiritual status or attainment, rather than used as tools for humble service for others, then conflict naturally follows. The core temptation to the first and Second Adam [Christ], and by extension to all of us, was to use spiritual knowledge and power to accredit one's independent and exalted religious status, instead of through them rendering glory, obedience and service to God. Spiritual gifts are powerful weapons against the kingdom of darkness; but misapplied in evidentialist polemics they can wound and destroy the people of God.

This charismata, then, reflect the very nature of God, who does not share his glory with another. Similarly, God is a Spirit of power, "who changeth not." If the church has "begun in the

Spirit," let us not attempt to change God's methods to complete our course in the weakness of human flesh. Since it is the Father's pleasure to "give good gifts to them who ask Him," it must be our pleasure to receive them humbly.[7]

I want to wrap up with a testimony from Kaisa, a young woman who stepped out in faith and saw God work through her to impact the lives of many in a country that is closed to Christianity. Kaisa went through my ministry school and was an intern for a time. Today Kaisa is leading evangelistic trips into the interior of Asia with many people coming to Christ. Making the decision not to marry, she has dedicated her life to Christ's service. Kaisa is Finnish and her story that follows begins and ends in Finland.

I got radically saved in August 1998 and received a call to full-time ministry with a focus on missions and evangelism. A year later, God started speaking to me about China, and so I began to make plans and find out how to get there. God had told me to work at an orphanage. Someone introduced me to a lady who was working far out in the western part of China on the Tibetan Plateau, and I knew this was the right connection. She, however, didn't have connections with orphanages. I told her that the Lord had told me to work at an orphanage and asked if she knew of any. She said there was one in the city where she lived, but they were not taking any foreigners due to the BBC documentaries about Chinese orphanages that had spread all over the world and put China in a very bad light. I had heard from God and was convinced this was my assignment, so I just trusted that He would make a way.

This woman felt there was no harm in asking, which she did. We prayed a lot and a miracle happened. I received a positive response and was welcomed to come and work as a volunteer starting in June 2000. I prepared myself, got my passport and visa ready, and then in May I got a message telling me the orphanage had a new leader and this person didn't want any foreigners there. I had just quit a well-paying job in my home country and moved my belongings to my parents' house in order to start my first adventure with God in China.

I was a very young Christian but had gotten deeply rooted and grounded in the Word of God during the first two years of my walk with Jesus, and I knew how to pray things through, so I decided to win this battle together with the Lord. With lots of prayer and faith and trust in God that nothing is impossible for Him when we obey His voice, I left for China without knowing what to do there. I was twenty-seven years old at that time and had never been on any kind of an outreach or mission trip, and now suddenly I was totally on my own and on my way to the unknown because I felt God had called me. I arrived in China and was able to live with a missionary who connected me with a medical team for a month so I would have something to do. I traveled with them just helping and serving. During this time, I fasted and prayed and proclaimed that the doors to this orphanage would open up again in the name of Jesus.

During the last day of the medical outreach, I heard that one of the participants was going to take something to that particular orphanage. I asked if I could join her and together the two of us went and spent about an hour there. We got to meet some of the children. As we were entertaining the kids, I saw someone standing in the hallway and was told that she was the new director. I walked up to her, introduced myself, and said I was offered a volunteer position there and asked whether I could still start. I said I was willing to do anything—clean the toilets or whatever they needed help for. She looked at me as if she was hypnotized and said, "Of course you can help. When can you start?" God opened up the way for me after all, as I had believed He would!

I worked in that place of total hopelessness for six months. My assignment was to take care of the most severely handicapped children. I realized right away that these kids had no future. And I also realized that I was powerless to change their destinies. I wasn't able to communicate with them because I didn't speak the language. The atmosphere in that place was demonic and depressive. Every child had a desperate look in their eyes. They all longed for love and attention but were just ignored, basically just barely kept alive. Many times I talked to the boss about how she could sign the home up for an adoption program. I was convinced that at least the healthy children would have a chance to get adopted if she made this one crucial move. She didn't seem to pay attention or care. Finally, I left China very discouraged, feeling like a loser who wasn't able to make any difference for those children, convinced that I had not heard from God and that the whole thing with China and the orphanage had just been my own imagination. I returned to my home country disillusioned and defeated with just one question ringing in my head: *What was this whole thing all about, God?*

Eight months went by, and then one day I received a letter from a lady I didn't know. She wanted to know whether I was the Kaisa who worked in that particular orphanage as a volunteer. She had contacted all the people under that same name in order to find me because she had great news. She told me that she adopted a girl from that orphanage and invited me to come and visit them. I couldn't believe it! I had thought the whole time that my contribution in that orphanage had zero impact and that I wasn't able to help the children and change their destinies in any way at all. I thought the director had just politely smiled at my enthusiasm. How wrong I had been! She had listened to me and done what I had proposed.

I immediately traveled to the city where this lady lived. I couldn't believe what I saw. The child who had been adopted from the orphanage was one I knew well, and she knew me. We had seen each other there every day. Now she had a home, a mother, and a sister in my home country. She had a future and all the possibilities to hear the gospel too. Soon after this, I started hearing similar stories. One story after the other followed of how children from that orphanage were adopted all over the world into wonderful homes, many into Christian homes.

God has a good sense of humor! Out of all the possible places in the world, He placed two girls from the very orphanage where I had worked in China into my hometown in Finland, into a well-known family that has had impact on the whole nation of Finland and even beyond. All in all, destinies of countless children from China have been changed because of the step of obedience I took twenty years ago.

As a twenty-seven-year-old, relatively fresh and inexperienced believer, this was a lesson that has had a lasting impact on me and become one of the cornerstones of my faith and walk with God. It taught me what obedience means—radical, immediate, complete obedience when God speaks. When He speaks, we had better do what He says even if it goes against our understanding, even if all the people around us oppose us and question the whole thing, even if it seems impossible and circumstances are against us and all doors seem to close. Even if we don't see immediate results or fruit of our labor, we had better obey in faith. When we do, enormous blessings will follow us, and we will reap the beautiful fruit of righteousness. I can only say with confidence that it is always worth it to obey God.

I love Kaisa's story and her willingness to trust God and go in faith. Her story, and the others in this book, give powerful witness to the truth and reality that the supernatural power of God, found in Scripture and displayed in miracles and signs and wonders, has not ended. In fact, as you will see, the miraculous is needed as much today as it was two thousand years ago, when God took His power and glory and through a handful of disciples spread the gospel to all the known world.

Before we begin our journey of following the threads of the miraculous that God has woven into His Word, I am extending an invitation, an exhortation, to take the content of this journey and bring it into your walk as a citizen of heaven who is commissioned to advance God's kingdom on the earth right here, right now. I want you to better understand the full redemptive value of the cross of Jesus. I want your understanding of the gospel to be enlarged with powerful implications not only for the next life but for this life as well.

ONE

TWENTY-FIRST-CENTURY DISCIPLESHIP AND THE SUPERNATURAL

MIRACLES, HEALING, SIGNS AND WONDERS AS found in Scripture have not ceased. I say this with confidence based on personal experience from fifty years of ministry, ten years of biblical and theological education, many years of studying church history, and the recorded experience of the mission field since the beginning of the twentieth century and continuing today in the twenty-first century.

In Acts 1:8, before Jesus' ascension, He told His disciples the means by which they were to fulfill their commission of spreading the gospel and teaching the new believers all that He had taught them. Jesus said, "You shall receive power when the Holy Spirit has come upon you; and you shall be witnesses to Me in Jerusalem, and in all Judea and Samaria, and to the end of the earth" (NKJV).

The church has often focused on fulfilling the Great Commission to make disciples, as given by Christ in Matthew 28:19–20, but does not connect the need for the power of the Holy Spirit to fulfill it. It is as if we forgot that Christ demonstrated the kingdom of God through the power of God as well as taught about it with words.[1] According to Scripture, we are called to do no less.

> I will not venture to speak of anything except what Christ has accomplished through me to bring the Gentiles to obedience—by word and deed, by the power of signs and wonders, by the power of the Spirit of God—so that from Jerusalem and all the way around to Illyricum I have fulfilled the ministry of the gospel of Christ. (Rom. 15:18–19 ESV)

> I came to you in weakness with great fear and trembling. My message and my preaching were not with wise and persuasive words, but with a demonstration of the Spirit's power, so that your faith might not rest on human wisdom, but on God's power. (1 Cor. 2:3–5)

> The kingdom of God is not a matter of talk but of power. (1 Cor. 4:20)

When the power of the Holy Spirit is connected to the commission to advance the kingdom, that commission is accomplished exponentially. The healings, deliverances, and other signs and wonders demonstrate that the kingdom of God is at hand. Church history up to the present day reveals this, showing us how the Holy Spirit's power is integrally connected to missions. You can read more about this in my book *Supernatural Missions*.[2] One of the primary purposes of the miracles of Jesus, which are also referred to as His works, is to bring people to faith in Jesus, resulting in the new believers being filled with the Holy Spirit so they, too, can advance the kingdom of God on the earth through the power and authority given to them. Jesus has come from God to reveal God. Jesus is the incarnation of God—the second person of the Trinity. He is the pioneer of our faith. In 1 Corinthians 4:16–17, Paul told new believers: "I urge you, then, be imitators of me. That is why I sent you Timothy . . . to remind you of my ways in Christ" (ESV). Again, in 1 Corinthians 11:1, Paul wrote, "Follow my example, as I follow the example of Christ." This is the biblical understanding of discipleship. It is not limited to knowing what the Master taught, but also involves following the Master's example of how to live and what to do. With this in mind, discipleship must include doing what He commands. His commission to us is a command to declare the gospel of the kingdom of heaven and to heal the sick, cast out demons, raise the dead, and preach the good news to the poor.[3]

As we study the role of the supernatural in the church, we find that it has a biblical aspect, a historical aspect, and a missiological aspect. The biblical aspect will be laid out in the remainder of this book. Ramsay MacMullen, emeritus professor of history at Yale University, emphasized that the primary reason people came to faith in Jesus during the first four hundred years of Christianity was the signs and wonders and the healings and deliverances worked by the early church.[4] Francis MacNutt's books *Healing* and *Healing Reawakening*, and my *School of Healing and Impartation 1 Workbook*, point out the importance of healing throughout the history of the church. Today, in the twenty-first century, this is the existential truth for almost all Muslims and other majority world people who are turning to Christ, as well as a host of other people groups world-wide, including first-world people.

Matt Scott is presently in my physical healing course at Global

Awakening Theological Seminary. Matt was at one time a senior sales representative for an orthopedic implant company. In 2011 he founded The Gathering Place Church in Alabama, beginning with his family in their living room. In summer 2019 he resigned his sales rep position to serve full time as the lead pastor at The Gathering Place. In December of that year his church had experienced an unexpected outpouring of the power of God while in a season of praying and fasting and began to see healings on a weekly basis. They now have had more than two hundred documented healings. In the eight years prior to this, their church rarely saw any signs of physical healings. The following testimony is from Matt.

On my second trip to India, I encountered a situation that challenged my theology pertaining to healing. At the time of this trip, I believed that healing was the byproduct of faith. I thought that it was a benefit offered to believers and was subsequent to justification—saving faith.

While on my trip, one of the local pastors invited me to come with him to a village where I was asked to share my testimony, share the gospel, and offer an opportunity for unbelievers to accept Christ. After sharing my testimony and completing my gospel presentation, I asked if anyone wanted to accept Jesus Christ. No one responded. I was disheartened by the lack of interest.

But just as we were about to thank them for their time and dismiss ourselves, one of the people came forward and said, "Please pray for me. I am deaf in left ear, and almost deaf in right ear." I thought to myself, *God, should I pray healing over someone who did not accept an invitation to follow You? If they did not have faith to accept Jesus, they cannot possibly have faith for Jesus to heal them.* But oddly I felt the Lord impress upon me to pray for his healing. I must admit that at this point I lacked faith for his healing and felt that the man's faith was minimal at best. But regardless, we prayed.

No sooner than I had said the words, "Come, Holy Spirit," the man began to squint as if in pain and then grabbed his ears with both hands. Immediately his eyes popped open and he looked around the room in shock. I didn't know if his condition was better or worse. Then all of a sudden he shouted in his native tongue, "I can hear!" Everyone in the room cheered and then he ran out of the room. I was very confused. I wanted to lead him to the person who healed him (Jesus), but he ran out before we could talk.

In a matter of two minutes, the man returned with a friend who was also deaf. He said, "Pray for her. She's deaf too." We prayed and her ears opened as well! They both ran out and went to retrieve another person who was deaf. God opened the third person's ears as well! In a matter of ten minutes, God had healed three people who did not believe in Jesus or originally have faith for Jesus to heal them. And as previously stated, my faith was minimal at best. What was going on?

At that point the Indian pastor began to speak. He talked for five minutes in their language. While I did not know what he was saying, I could tell that they were engaged. They were all nodding their heads in agreement. When finished, he looked at me and said, "They are now ready to accept Christ."

I said, "Which ones?"

He said, "All of them."

It was the easiest salvation prayer I have ever led. Without hesitation, all twenty-five people in the room accepted Jesus.

The next day we returned, and news had spread concerning the healings. We prayed for many more individuals. Some were healed on the spot and some were not. Regardless, in less than three days more than one hundred people accepted Jesus in that village! This event challenged and eventually changed my theology that required faith for healing. Many times since this event, God has prompted me to begin my evangelistic efforts not with my story, or the gospel presentation, but with praying for the sick. I am finding that in many cases God will heal people's bodies first, then heal their souls second.

In one case I was invited to a home filled with many radical Muslims and Hindus. I was advised to break the ice by sharing stories about America and my culture, and then *if* received well to "carefully" communicate the gospel to them. But as I was about to begin, my attention was drawn to a man standing along the wall with a shoulder sling. I felt the Spirit of God say, *Begin by praying for his healing.* I asked my translator if this would be okay. He said, "Yes, but be careful not to say the name Jesus out loud in your prayer. These men are accustomed to healing prayers but may have problems with the name of Jesus."

At this point I was a little nervous, but decided to move forward with prayer. I began to pray by audibly saying, "God, I know that You love this man and You love all these in the room. Lord, the Enemy has deceived most of them into believing things that are false and things that will ultimately lead them to death. Will You please come now and show them Your love? Will You please heal this man and offer me an opportunity to introduce them to You?"

After the prayer the man just sat there. Everyone in the room was staring at the two of us. When I asked if he felt anything he said, "No."

My heart sank. I asked the Lord, *What now?*

I felt the Lord say, *Tell him to move it.* So I asked if he would move his shoulder a little to see if it still hurt. Very gently he began to move his shoulder. He moved it slowly from front to back. When he realized it was no longer in pain, he began to move it more. He moved it from side to side and then up and down. Finally he took the sling off and raised his hand over his head. The Lord had completely healed him! At that point a once-abrasive audience was very curious about what happened. After I told them about Jesus and God's love for them, they all accepted Christ.

Matt Scott and many others, such as Leif Hetland,[5] Heidi Baker,[6] and Robbie Dawkins,[7] are witnessing the supernatural power of God to bring, in Leif's case, more than one million unbelievers and people of other faiths to Jesus. The same is true of Heidi's ministry, and, in Robbie's case, hundreds, including Taliban members. These are exciting times for the church.

ADVANCING GOD'S KINGDOM ON THE EARTH

When I have an opportunity to teach on the subject of leadership—what it means to become a history maker or a powerful leader in the church—I emphasize two things. The first is the need for a powerful personal encounter with God that comes in the form of an impartation, a filling with His Holy Spirit that baptizes and sanctifies. The second is having a certainty regarding your destiny—a strong call from God. With these two things, you will have the grace, power, and faith to persevere in the face of great hardship. Without them you will not be able to fulfill His call on your life, for it is "'not by might nor by power, but by [God's] Spirit,' says the LORD" (Zech. 4:6). When you are willing and certain of your calling, His Spirit working in you can accomplish extraordinary things to advance His kingdom on the earth.

A great many revivalist evangelists in history were also healing evangelists. We see this from the great advance in missions at the beginning of the twentieth century and even more at the middle of the twentieth century, related to the role of healing evangelists who were touched in the revival of the late 1940s and early 1950s. This is also often the pattern throughout church history. Healing evangelists were heroes of the faith who heard and obeyed. It was the hearing of the word of the Lord that gave them faith to do mighty exploits in the name of the Lord. Revival is characterized by the power of God, when people are touched so powerfully that they yield their lives to the purposes of God (1 Thess. 1:5; Acts 1:8; 2:1–4; 4:23–33). The fruit of these outpourings of the Spirit is seen in salvations, new churches planted, and people called to crosscultural missions, among other things. Historic revival movements such as the First and Second Great Awakenings, the Welsh Revival, the Azusa Street Revival, the 1948 Healing Revival, and more recently the Billy Graham crusades, the Charismatic Renewal of 1960, the Jesus Movement, the Toronto Blessing, the Pensacola Revival, the Smithton Outpouring, and visitations at evangelical colleges in the last decade of the twentieth century—all have revealed the face of God in the power of the Holy Spirit. Millions have responded, daring to do what seems impossible.

An event called The Send in Brazil filled three stadiums in January 2020 with about 160,000 in attendance. I had the privilege of addressing all three stadiums simultaneously on the last night. This event was a call to the churches in Brazil to send forth the laborers into the harvest, to send out laborers to the lost, the poor, the marginalized, and to the nations.[8] I led a short impartation service, and many attested to being powerfully touched by the Holy Spirit. Many were healed during this one-day event. It was a demonstration that the younger generation realizes discipleship to Jesus involves *doing* the works He prepared in advance for us to walk in (Eph. 2:8–10). The Bible is never to be reduced to an ethical manual for living. It is so much more. Bible study is intended to lead to doing what the Bible tells us to do, which involves two kinds of fruit: the fruit of being (Gal. 5:22–23) and the fruit of doing (John 14:12–14).

The connection Jesus made between power and mission in Acts 1:8 is reflected in both Matthew's gospel (28:18–20) and Luke's gospel (24:45–49), with the promise of the Spirit connected to mission that was fulfilled in Luke's second volume, the book of Acts. Power in this context is a delegated authority from Jesus connected to the glory of God. We will study the relationship between glory and power in greater depth later, but for now it is sufficient to understand that miracles, signs, and wonders reveal God's glory. He is the source of this power to move in the miraculous. It is His energy working in us that powerfully produces compassion, love, faith, enabling grace, the ability to suffer, and perseverance for the advance of the gospel in the world.

Do power and the gifts exist for the church or for the mission?

I believe they exist primarily for the mission and are done through the church. It is important to remember that Christ died for the church; however, the church's job is to find other "sheep" and bring them into the fold (John 10:16), and to make known the manifold wisdom of God to the rulers and authorities in the heavenly places through the church (Eph. 3:10). A second question is, What is the primary purpose of the power of God? Is it to bear witness to the apostles and their teaching as evidence of correct doctrine, or to display God's compassion, love, and the nature of God? I believe it is the latter—the primary purpose of God's power is to be a continuing revelation of His love and an integral part of the presentation of the gospel that is proclaimed with signs following. In fact, this should be normative rather than exceptional in this time in the history of the church. While cessationism was the belief held by the vast majority of Protestants until the early part of the mid-nineteenth century, we now have witnessed more than 100 years of the latter-day outpouring of the Spirit upon His church. Furthermore, we are more than 150 years beyond the beginning of Protestants rediscovering the ministry of healing.

God's power working through us allows us to be a missional people the way the apostolic church was missional. Our apologetic for the faith is not based so much on reason but on the power of God as demonstrated by the apostle Paul, who wrote, "My message and my preaching were not with wise and persuasive words, but with a demonstration of the Spirit's power, so that your faith might not rest on human wisdom, but on God's power" (1 Cor. 2:4–5). Power evangelism as Jesus demonstrated it calls us to live in the fullness of His gospel. Christ in you *is* truly the hope of glory, the hope of miracles, the hope of power. How can we not have expectation for mighty things to happen through us when He is in us and His Spirit is on us? Yet, we must believe that He is in us, believe that He is bubbling up in us. We must understand that the living Christ lives in us. He is near, as close as our breath. We are called by Scripture, called by the living God, to take our belief beyond doctrines that have hindered us—beyond overemphasis on sovereignty, overemphasis on holiness, and even, dare I say it, an overemphasis on one's ability to have faith—and into the world so that all may know Him as Lord and Savior.

I pray God will develop in you both faith and hunger to grow in your ability to recognize His communications to you. I pray you will respond as I did when, in the 1970s, I read testimonies of divine appointments with Christians and cried out in prayer, "God, if this is possible today, if You still communicate with people like this, if it is possible to live this kind of a Christian life—that is what I want." Following this prayer I experienced a greater hunger and thirst to know God, to walk in His will, to have divine appointments, and to hear the Holy Spirit's communications. May it be for you also.

Join me as together we follow the threads God has woven into His Word to show us the connections between obedience and intimacy; intimacy and revelation; revelation and faith; faith and healing, miracles, signs, and wonders; healing, miracles, signs, wonders and the glory of the Father and the Son in the power of the Holy Spirit.

TWO

SIGNS, WONDERS, AND MIRACLES IN JESUS' MINISTRY

I AM THANKFUL FOR MANY THINGS, NOT THE LEAST of which is my Baptist heritage with its strong emphasis on Scripture. Throughout my personal pilgrimage to better know and experience the triune God, Scripture has been my foundation. Thus, it makes perfect sense for us to pick up one of God's threads and begin our journey to a greater understanding of the supernatural life of Jesus and its implications for our lives today as believers, in the pages of the four gospels—Matthew, Mark, Luke, and John. These gospels are replete with miracles, healings, deliverances, signs, and wonders. Jesus was always busy about the work of His Father, and that work was characterized by the miraculous. As you read the Gospels, particularly the gospel of John, you see that Jesus didn't go about randomly doing miracles with an occasional raising of the dead. By His very nature, Jesus healed from a place of intimacy with the Father and with great compassion. It was from this intimacy that He received revelation of what the Father was saying and doing so that He could partner with God. When the religious authorities asked why He had healed a lame man on the Sabbath, He replied that it was what He saw His Father doing (John 5:2–17). That kind of radical obedience to the Father was costly for Jesus.

So what does radical obedience from a place of intimacy with God involve, and why is it important for us as believers today? As I mentioned in the introduction, understanding the supernatural life of Jesus shines light on the liberal and cessationist beliefs that are having an impact upon the church. These beliefs have resulted in a poor model of discipleship with no emphasis upon what Jesus modeled, taught, and commissioned the church to do—which is to heal the sick, cast out demons, and bring good news to the poor (Matt. 10:8). This commission to believers begins with intimacy, which opens the door to revelation and in turn builds a confident faith that allows the miraculous works of the kingdom of God to flow on the earth through believers like you and me. The inbreaking of the kingdom of God on the earth—"on earth as it is in heaven"— should be daily in our prayers, per Jesus' teaching (Matt. 6:10). It is this flow of the supernatural from God to humanity that draws humankind to the Father.

The word *miracles* is mentioned twenty-seven times in the Bible (NIV). The term *signs* appears seventy-two times, and *signs and wonders* occurs twenty-one times in the Bible (NIV). The gospels of Matthew, Mark, and Luke, known as the Synoptic Gospels, bring us many of the same stories of the life and ministry of Jesus, often in similar sequence. The gospel of John, on the other hand, brings us additional events from the life of Jesus not found in the Synoptic Gospels, and with a different emphasis. John focuses intently on the divinity of Jesus as the manifestation and expression of God in the world, with an emphasis on the intimacy and obedience of Jesus in performing miracles. John records seven miracles in contrast to Matthew's twenty-nine miracles, Mark's twenty-four miracles, and Luke's twenty-three miracles. Six of the seven miracles in John are unique to his gospel. Biblical scholars tend to agree that John, known as the "beloved disciple," enjoyed a deeply intimate relationship with Jesus. This deep intimacy is further reflected in the book of Revelation, penned, most scholars believe, by John.

In the Gospels we find some forty accounts of both physical and mental healings performed by Jesus, not including those places in the Gospels that record scores or even hundreds of people being healed, or those instances when He raised the dead. Nor does this count include natural miracles such as multiplication of food, calming storms, walking on water, turning water to wine, or finding a coin in a fish's mouth. In fact, according to John, the Gospels only give us a smattering of the miracles performed by Jesus during His three years of ministry (John 2:23). Yet, all these miracles pale in comparison to the greatest miracle of all, the resurrection of Jesus from the dead. This was not only a miracle of resuscitation but also of glorification, for surely all the miracles that flow from heaven are to give glory to God. The resurrection miracle begins with another miracle: the incarnation. "The Word became flesh, and dwelt among us, and we beheld His glory, the glory as of the only begotten of the Father, full of grace and truth" (John 1:14 NKJV). We have been given the beloved Son of God, in whom the Father is well pleased, as the author and perfecter of our faith, a faith that flows from revelation, which comes from intimacy with the One who loves. The great gift of Jesus is worthy of our confident faith and obedience to His will and specific directives in our lives.

John Wimber, in appendix D of his book *Power Healing*, gives an excellent overview of the healing ministry of Jesus. In it, he noted eleven distinct ways in which the miracles of Jesus occurred. These are in order of frequency mentioned: (1) word spoken, twenty-one references; (2) touched by Jesus, thirteen references; (3) drove out demons; nine references; (4) the faith of another, eight references; (5) the person's faith, six references; (6) the prayer of another, five references; (7) preaching of Jesus, four references; (8) teaching of Jesus, four references; (9) Jesus moved with compassion, four references; (10) touching Jesus, four references; and in last position, (11) person touches Jesus, two references.[1] The majority of the miracles recorded in the Gospels note at least one of these ways, but not all of them. We often see these eleven, and many more, reflected in the history of the miraculous in the church, especially today. Why is this important? As we minister in Jesus' name, in the power of the Holy Spirit, these distinct ways can serve as indicators that God is at work and can inspire others to seek healing. Let's look at this through the lens of a twenty-first-century testimony from Jessika, and then from Scripture.

Jessika is a Global Awakening Theological Seminary student in my eight-week class on healing. (Before taking this class, some students have never had a word of knowledge or seen a healing when they prayed.) Jessika is a lay person who currently lives and ministers on the mission field, traveling to train leaders and missionaries in how to walk in the supernatural and have sustainable, healthy leadership. She began her mission work in South Africa at the age of eighteen, went from there to the Congo, and is now living in Brazil. She is hosted by the largest traditional Baptist church in Brazil with an average weekly attendance of eighteen thousand. This church was powerfully impacted by several of our team's teaching conferences on healing. The pastor's wife and another key staff person, a psychologist, came to our Summer Global Intensive in Mechanicsburg, Pennsylvania, to receive more intense training. Jessika is able to be a student at Global Awakening Theological Seminary because the classes are available online. The following is Jessika's testimony of healing and deliverance through a word of knowledge.

I felt a pain in my knee as I was walking up the stairs to my office. My immediate thought was that this was a word of knowledge for someone that I would encounter that day. A few minutes later I was called to make a house visit to a family in our church. As we walked into the house, I felt the pain in my left knee again. This was confirmation to me that the word of knowledge was for someone in the house. I could not decide if the word was for the man or woman present, so I asked if either of them had any pain in their knee. The man responded that he had a mild pain in his knee and then explained that he had been in an accident and had fallen off a truck. The accident severely damaged his back and caused problems in his knee as well, leaving him unable to work.

I asked if he could explain to me what happened with his knee. He said that when he fell off the truck his knee twisted in a way that has caused reoccurring mild pain. I asked if he had any unforgiveness toward the man who had caused the accident. He said that he did not. Then I asked, on a scale of one to ten, what level of pain his knee was in at that moment. He said it was only a two, but his back was a ten. I decided to pray for the knee first because that was the word of knowledge I had received. I asked if it was okay for me to put my hand on his knee, which he agreed to. I explained that I was going to pray for him and asked him not to pray while I was praying, but instead to pay attention to his body as I prayed. I asked him to be aware of any changes that he might feel in his body or in the room.

As I prayed, I felt specifically that I needed to break trauma from the accident off him. Although he said he did not need to forgive anyone, I could sense that there was extreme disappointment from the effects of the accident. I decided to start by dealing with the trauma and then pray for healing.

I began the prayer by inviting Holy Spirit to come and touch him. I waited a few seconds to discern if I felt Holy Spirit moving in any particular direction. At this point I did not feel anything, and so I began the prayer to break off trauma. I commanded any trauma from the accident to leave and any lingering effects of the trauma in his body to leave. After this I commanded the pain in his knee to leave and declared complete healing over the knee. I did this twice before pausing to see if Holy Spirit was saying anything else. At this point I personally was not feeling anything or seeing any change in him, so I decided to re-interview him.

I asked if there was any change in the level of pain in his knee. He said that there had been no change. I asked if he felt anything at all, to which he responded that he did not. At this moment I felt another word of knowledge about witchcraft. I asked him if he had been involved in witchcraft, and he said that he had not, but his ex-wife had been. I felt led to continue to pursue this further. I asked if he had anything in his house that was symbolic of witchcraft. He then told me that the previous week his current wife had burned various articles of witchcraft that had been in the house since before his divorce.

I then asked if he had repented of allowing the witchcraft in his home, and he said he had not. At this point I led him in repenting of the witchcraft he allowed in his home, telling him to repent of these sins specifically, which he did. I instructed him to ask Jesus to forgive him of his sins and cleanse him from all unrighteousness. I then asked if he felt he could forgive his ex-wife for participating in witchcraft and bringing it into his home, which he said he could. He then began to verbally forgive his wife. Finally, I asked him to renounce all the witchcraft that had been done and all articles of witchcraft that were brought into their home. I then asked if he felt anything in this moment and he said that he felt "lighter." At that point, I decided to pray for his back instead of returning to the knee.

Again, I asked Holy Spirit to come and touch him. When I placed my hand on his back, I began to feel heat. I noticed that he began to cry and that Holy Spirit was touching him. Before I began praying again, he started moving his hips and stretching his back. At this point I knew Holy Spirit was already healing his back, so I partnered with what the Spirit was doing. I prayed multiple times, "more, more, more." After about thirty seconds, I commanded all trauma to leave his body, then commanded healing in his back. The heat in my hand began to increase, and he began sobbing. I asked Holy Spirit to continue to touch him and waited one or two minutes to allow him to encounter Holy Spirit.

I told him that I could see God was touching him and he nodded in agreement. I asked where his pain level was, and he said that the pain was gone in his back and in his knee. I asked what he had felt in his body. He said that he felt heat start in his back where I placed my hand and then move throughout his entire body. I asked how his heart was feeling. He said that he felt "peace" and "relief." I encouraged him to see his doctor to have a scan done of his back. All this was done via translation.

Jessika received a word of knowledge from God via a physical pain in her knee. God wanted to heal someone, and He communicated this to Jessika, who has learned how to hear from God and knows to be obedient and act on what God is doing. Her faith and obedience resulted in a man receiving healing and deliverance. Her willingness to share her testimony means that God will receive glory and others will be encouraged to both minister healing and receive healing. First Chronicles 16:12 tells us, "Remember the wonders he has done, his miracles, and the judgments he pronounced." Revelation 19:10 says, "The testimony of Jesus is the spirit of prophecy" (ESV).

As believers, one aspect of our work in the world is to proclaim the testimony of Jesus as we give glory to God, whose Holy Spirit brings the initiative for prophecy (Rev. 1:2, 9). In Luke 8:40–48 we find the story of the woman with the issue of blood, who upon touching the *edge of Jesus' cloak* was healed. At the end of Matthew 14, we get a glimpse of how impactful this woman's healing was. "And when the men of that place recognized Jesus, they sent word to all the surrounding country. People brought all their sick to him and begged him to let the sick just touch the *edge of his cloak*, and all who touched it were healed" (vv. 35–36, emphasis mine). As word of the woman's healing spread, faith for healing rose up in others who then did as she had done—they went to Jesus and touched the edge of His cloak—and they, too, were healed. Her testimony caused others to have faith for a similar healing wrought in the same way—touching the edge of His cloak.

God's desire is that each one of us would have a more bountiful, triumphant, supernatural lifestyle. This involves being both the recipient of His healing touch on our bodies and minds and conduits of His miraculous works so others may also experience His touch. It all begins with intimacy. In the next chapter we will examine some aspects of Jesus' Upper Room Discourse from John 13:31–16:33 to better understand what intimacy with the Father looks like as it relates to the ministry of healing and the ramifications of such intimacy in the lives of believers.

THREE

INTIMACY AND THE
MINISTRY OF HEALING

IN THE UPPER ROOM DISCOURSE (JOHN 13:31–16:33),
Jesus gave His final, crucial words to His disciples before His death.
There are many concepts within these passages of Scripture that
highlight intimacy as it relates to the ministry of healing. The
concepts are simple but profound and contain some of the most
insightful portions of the Bible regarding intimacy. In these passages
Jesus reveals how Christians are meant to live a more abundant,
victorious, supernatural lifestyle through intimacy with the Father.
As I read through these passages, I hear Jesus giving His disciples
the secrets of His power and His relationship with the Father that
grew out of His obedience. Because Jesus was perfectly obedient to
the Father, there was nothing that ever hindered His ability to see
and hear what the Father was doing.

As we begin, I want to bring clarity to what I understand Jesus
was saying regarding *works* in this passage. Some read John 13:31–
16:33 and interpret that Jesus is referring to *works* we can do in our

natural ability. However, if you read this passage in its context, you will see that Jesus is not just talking about works we can do in our natural ability. He is also talking about works that take supernatural enablement, supernatural grace. These kinds of works can only be accomplished in the power of the Holy Spirit, and when they are done, they bring glory to God. Jesus wanted His disciples to understand this truth, and He wants the church to understand it also.

Let's pick up the thread in John 14:10–14. Jesus was teaching on the topic of glorifying the Father. In these verses He made the connection between intimacy (that flows out of obedience), healing (that flows out of God's presence), and bringing glory to God. He was teaching the disciples that the Father receives glory through works done in His (Jesus') name. Tied in with the aspect of obedience is a strong trinitarian emphasis—through Jesus the Son, we have access to the Father and the Holy Spirit. In this trinitarian emphasis we find the connection between authority and power, and between presence and joy. In other words, power to operate in miracles, signs, and wonders is related to the authority He gives us.

The authority was given to believers at the commissionings of the Twelve, the seventy-two, and in the post-resurrection Great Commission of Matthew 28:18–20. Jesus told His disciples to wait in Jerusalem for the power to come upon them by the Holy Spirit. The Holy Spirit enables the presence of the triune God in us, and that presence brings us power to glorify Him, which in turn brings fullness of joy and pleasures forevermore (Ps. 16:11). With His presence in us, we (the church) are able to bring God glory through the miraculous, just as Jesus did.

As I write this, a testimony from my friend Leif Hetland comes to mind. In 2010 Leif took a large team from America, Europe, and

Australia to Africa. A few years earlier, a couple of South Africans had climbed to the top of Kilimanjaro and prayed, and they saw a vision of the glory of God. His glory was touching Kilimanjaro, the highest point in Africa, and it was spreading a revival fire from Kilimanjaro all the way throughout the continent of Africa to the Middle East and Israel. Based upon that prophecy, as well as input from intercessors who had been praying, a movement known as the African Call was organized to bring unity among churches and different denominations in the region around Kilimanjaro. Leif brought a large team, both for worship and to minister healing and deliverance.

About eleven thousand people were present at one of the large gatherings. Worship ended, followed by an amazing introduction from the African leaders of the event who lavished a high level of honor on Leif, who was about to speak. This was during a season when Leif was learning to be more sensitive to the Holy Spirit. However, he wasn't ready for what was about to happen. As he approached the microphone, he felt a whisper from the Holy Spirit. It was not an external voice but rather the clear internal voice of the Holy Spirit. As he was hearing this whisper, he was also sensing tension in the air from the large, noisy crowd. Wanting to be sensitive to the Spirit, he pressed in to try and hear more clearly what the Spirit was saying. Immediately, he was taken back in his memory to a song he used to sing as a child in Sunday school in Norway. He hadn't sung this song since he was a child—hadn't even thought about it. Yet, as he pressed in, he felt the Holy Spirit whispering, *I want you to sing this song.*

Leif will be the first to tell you that he is not a singer. In fact, he dislikes his singing voice so much that not only will he not sing in public if he can possibly help it, but he doesn't even like to hear himself sing when he is alone. But he was hearing the whisper of the Spirit to sing the song in Norwegian, which nobody present spoke except Leif. It would be altogether strange and weird to do something like that. *Was it the devil or God?* he wondered. But why would the devil want him to sing a sweet song about Jesus? Leif knew it wasn't his flesh because he strongly disliked singing, and it likely wasn't the devil, so he figured it must be the Holy Spirit. Yet, even so, he hesitated to act on what he was hearing. Then he heard it again, *I want you to sing this song for the people.* Despite the internal tension, rather than arguing with the Holy Spirit, he decided to obey.

Stepping to the microphone, he began to sing the song in Norwegian. "Father, I have this prayer in my heart that I want to be more like Jesus. And that you, Jesus, need to grow and I need to become smaller." As he sang, the translator began to look quizzically at him and so did the people. Even Leif's team didn't understand what was going on. Though he had forgotten most of the words, relieved that he had been obedient, he was about to move on and begin his talk when he heard the Holy Spirit whisper, *I want you to sing it again.* Standing there before the microphone with everyone looking at him, he felt frustration and irritation trying to rise up within him. The whole thing was so uncomfortable, yet struggling to be obedient to what he thought must be the voice of the Holy Spirit, he sang it a second time. Again, everyone was looking at him, wondering what in the world was going one. Things were beginning to feel very strange.

Then he heard the Spirit's whisper a third time, *Sing it again.* Struggling to be obedient and not knowing what else to do, Leif lifted his voice a third time, but it was void of any excitement, almost melancholic. A feeling of oppression began to creep over him as he saw the puzzlement on people's faces. All sense of excitement had left the room. There at the microphone, feeling like he wanted to run and hide, he heard it again, a fourth time—the still, small whisper of the Holy Spirit saying, *Do it again.* Knowing that there was no turning back at that point, just as he was about to lift his voice a fourth time to sing, a presence came into the place. It touched Leif first and he began to weep as the glory of God's presence came upon him. Then God's presence swept across the stage and out to the people. Suddenly masses of people were violently shaking under the presence of God. It felt as if the Holy Spirit was saying, *Leif, let Me take over. You did your part, now let Me do mine.* Mass healing took place, with seven thousand people healed. All kinds of healings and miracles took place along with mass deliverance. Leif's friend Tom Hauser, who had brought a deliverance team of twenty-six people, set up a deliverance tent, which quickly filled up as the Lord took people deep into freedom.

When I talked to Leif about this experience, he said it was a lesson he will never forget. He obeyed with faith, and the result was that God received so much glory. Many lives were changed. People were saved, healed, and delivered when he obeyed and let the Holy Spirit take over the meeting. He's quick to say that the singing is not something he would want to do again unless the Holy Spirit asked him to. Yet, he wants to be available and make adjustments as the Spirit directs him and obey whatever He says.

ANYONE WITH FAITH IN JESUS

Before we go further into the issue of presence, I want to take a moment to highlight the importance of faith to the promises of

Jesus. Many people, when they read verse 12 in John 14—"Very truly I tell you, whoever believes in me will do the works I have been doing, and they will do even greater things than these, because I am going to the Father"—wonder whom Jesus is speaking to. Some say that He was only speaking to the apostles. But when we examine this verse we see that is not the case. He doesn't say, "I tell you the truth, the *apostles* who have faith in me will do what I have been doing." He says, "*Anyone* who has faith in me . . ." Many have tried to take the words of Jesus here and say that they apply only to the elders of the church, but that is not what Jesus said.

I have a friend, a chiropractor, who is an elder in a church near my home. One of his employees is a Christian. I was talking to this particular employee one day and asked if she prayed for the people they treated. Her response was, "Oh, no. I would never pray for anybody." I said, "Well, why not?" She replied, "Because in James 5 it says to let the elders pray for the sick. We believe in healing, and we let the elders of our church pray for the sick, but only the elders."

This is a common view held by many in the church, but it is not what Jesus said in John 14:12. He was speaking to all of us (*anyone*). And if we examine this passage a little closer, we see that Jesus attached a condition to His promise. He tells us that we must have *faith* in Him if we are to do the works He did. Faith is the condition needed for this promise to become reality. We must be careful not to emphasize the promises and skip the conditions— that is not biblical. Oh, and by the way, church elders should have a special grace for healing because it is in their job description in James 5:14–15. It is also notable that James 5:16 seems to enlarge the scope of who can pray for healing: "Therefore confess your sins to each other and pray for each other so that you may be healed. The prayer of a righteous person is powerful and effective." The "each other" of 5:16 seems to enlarge the ability to pray beyond the elders. And it is interesting to note the qualifier in this verse, "righteous."

THE TRINITARIAN EMPHASIS

If we are to do the works Jesus did and bring glory to the Father, we need His presence in us. Let's look closer at John 14:15 to better understand what Jesus is saying about the trinitarian aspect of God's presence in us and its relationship to the miraculous.

> "If you love me, you will keep my commandments. And I will ask the Father, and he will give you another Helper, to be with you forever, even the Spirit of truth, whom the world cannot receive, because it neither sees him nor knows him. You know him, for he dwells with you and will be in you.
>
> "I will not leave you as orphans; I will come to you. Yet a little while and the world will see me no more, but you will see me. Because I live, you also will live. In that day you will know that I am in my Father, and you in me, and I in you. Whoever has my commandments and keeps them, he it is who loves me. And he who loves me will be loved by my Father, and I will love him and manifest myself to him." Judas (not Iscariot) said to him, "Lord, how is it that you will manifest yourself to us, and not to the world?" Jesus answered him, "If anyone loves me, he will keep my word, and my Father will love him, and we will come to him and make our home with him." (John 14:15–23 ESV)

Listen to what Jesus is saying. He is telling us that the person who loves Him will obey Him, because obedience is the overflow of an intimate, loving relationship rooted in love for the One who saved us by grace through faith alone. And to the one who obeys Him, He will reveal Himself through the Holy Spirit, who will come to live in us. Let's examine that last sentence more closely. "And we will come to him and make our home with him." How is that possible? What Jesus is saying is that when the Holy Spirit comes into you, the Father and the Son are in you as well because of the nature of the Trinity. *There is a relationship between intimacy with Jesus and the manifestation (or revelation) of Jesus and visitation (or habitation) of the Father and the Son with us by the Holy Spirit.* The question is then raised, "How do we get a habitation?" Simple! The habitation is "Jesus in us." This habitation, this "Jesus in us," is a reality for everyone who is truly saved. But, many times persons do not understand how to recognize the *ways of God*, and because of this lack of knowledge or understanding do not recognize God's communications in their lives. But sometimes we grieve the One in us to such an extent that some of His revelation gets blocked.

FRIENDS OF GOD, NOT SERVANTS

By the way, let's not think that the only things God wants us to hear are His "orders" telling us what to do. We might tend to think that way sometimes—that if we receive something from God it has to be for a purpose, for some work for God. That is a servant mentality, bunkhouse thinking, prodigal child thinking, not the mindset of a friend. Jesus calls us friends, not servants (John 15:15). This doesn't mean that we are not servants, a very common and favorite term for the apostle Paul. But we are more than servants; we are friends. This position is built on the former position of being servants. Friends receive revelation. Friends know the Master's business. And how does Jesus make His Father's business known to us? By the activity of the Spirit, what we call the "gifts." My Baptist grandma used to say, "God is talking to me. God showed me." Well, God continues to give us directions today. Sometimes He shows us things that tell us just how much He loves us until we are so overwhelmed by His love that all we can do is weep. Sometimes He shows us His joy, and at other times He will just say, *I want you to go here and do this.* When Jesus said "No longer do I call you servants, for a servant does not know what his master is doing; but I have called you friends, for *all things* that I heard from My Father I have made known to you," He was referring to *all* that He wants to reveal to us (John 15:15 NKJV, emphasis mine).

We can fall prey to the misconception that the only reason God would give us a revelation (a word of knowledge, or a prophecy, or a revelation that brings about inspiration) would be for the purpose of healing or as prophecy to encourage someone or insight to encourage us. However, that is not the case. Revelation given to us by God is not only to do something for Him. Oftentimes He is just speaking to us as a friend. He might give revelation to reveal a depth of insight into the love of the Father and the Son and the Holy Spirit, or to reveal the glory of each within the Trinity, or simply because He likes to interact with us. I have a great story to illustrate this point.

One of my former assistant pastors and his wife were on their way to visit their friends in another state. They were driving down the road when all of a sudden the Lord spoke to the wife and said, *Oh! By the way, when you get to your friend's house, they are going to have a new refrigerator.* The wife heard this just as clear as could be, but she didn't understand why God would tell her something like that.

It seemed to be a revelation with no purpose, no usefulness. She had just had one of the clearest revelations in her life and she didn't know what to do with it. And so, she asked the Lord, "Lord, why would You tell me that? What am I supposed to do with that?" The Lord's reply really surprised her. He said, *You can't do anything with it. I didn't tell you that because I wanted you to do something. I talk with you because I like to. Why does there have to be a purpose? You are My friend.*

When they arrived at their friend's house, they were ushered into the kitchen and with great excitement shown the new refrigerator. The pastor's wife said she had never been so excited to see a new appliance because at that moment she realized that God truly does enjoy His friendship with her—that He does take delight in their relationship. Isn't that a sweet story? I want that kind of relationship with God. I want to hear Him in that way, not just a "job order," a "do this for Me," but a relationship in which God simply likes to talk with me. That is intimacy.

THE REGENERATING WORK OF THE HOLY SPIRIT

If we desire this kind of intimacy, we must first understand its connection to obedience. Let's pick up the thread in John 14:15. Jesus said, "If you love me, keep my commands." We are not saved by obedience, but we can have greater intimacy with Jesus if we obey Him. If we start violating this request for obedience by saying yes to the sinful things we want to do and no to things the Spirit is leading us to do but we don't want to do, it will affect our intimacy and our revelation. Guilt hinders relationship. In John 14:16–17 Jesus shows us the connection between obedience and receiving the Holy Spirit. "I will ask the Father, and he will give you another advocate to help you and be with you forever—the Spirit of truth." Understand, this obedience is not possible apart from the renewing and regenerating work of the Holy Spirit in us. Then, in verses 21 and 23, we see obedience tied to intimacy and intimacy to the revelation of Jesus.

> "Whoever has my commands and keeps them is the one who loves me. The one who loves me will be loved by my Father, and I too will love them and show myself to them." . . . Jesus replied, "Anyone who loves me will obey my teaching. My Father will love them, and we will come to them and make our home with them."

I am not talking here about just the revelation of Jesus as in "I will reveal Myself to you." I am talking about revelation in the sense that God speaks to us. There are many in the church who adhere to a theology that says God does not speak to us anymore, that He no longer reveals things to us. But sometimes the theology that comes from our music is more accurate than that which comes from the pulpit. Take for instance the marvelous old hymn "In the Garden." The lyrics say, "And he walks with me and he talks with me and he tells me I am his own. And the joy we share as we tarry there, none other has ever known."[1] Jesus says, "My sheep listen to my voice; I know them, and they follow me" (John 10:27).

There really is communication between God and His people. We do not need to complicate it. When He tells us something or reveals something to us, we simply need to learn to accept it. Others may try to complicate the issue, but I say let's keep it simple. Here is a testimony from Caleb Roe, a Global Awakening Theological

Seminary student, that illustrates this concept. The son of a pastor, Caleb grew up in the church but had no desire to follow in his father's footsteps until he had an encounter with the Holy Spirit through a prophetic word. The profound nature of that encounter led him to quit his secular job and begin serving Jesus. He started out as a student pastor, and after fifteen years of growing and learning, he found himself leading the Dayton Vineyard Church established by his father in the early 1990s. The Vineyard Church is based on the ministry of John Wimber, whose message of taking the best of charismatic belief and balancing it with clear biblical teachings has always resonated with Caleb. Caleb strives to maintain the radical middle in ministry with a balance of Word and Spirit. He recalls:

While we were out to lunch, there was a young lady named Molly serving us. For most of the lunch she looked rather distressed. About halfway through the meal, I began wondering what was happening in her life, so I prayed and asked the Father to give me a prophetic word to share with her to cheer her up. After several minutes, I felt pain on the left side of my spine, about eight inches below my neck. When Molly brought our check, I said, "I'm a pastor at a local church, and sometimes God shows me things about people. I am wondering, do you have any pain in your back about eight inches below your neck?" A little shocked, she responded that she did.

When I asked her what was going on, she told me that she had minor scoliosis and that most days it doesn't bother her. But for some reason it was causing her a great deal of discomfort lately. When I asked if she had done anything to cause the injury, she responded that she had not. She had just awakened with the pain a few days ago and was hoping it would go away. Then I asked her if she had been dealing with anything heavy in her life that felt like a weight upon her shoulders. At that point, she began to weep in a way that I've noticed people do when the Holy Spirit begins to touch them. Through tears she told us that recently her life was feeling like a string of no-win scenarios and that she felt so hopeless. As she confessed this, she wept some more, with the Spirit resting on her.

There were two things going on with Molly that I thought God wanted to address. The first was that her back was damaged from scoliosis and in need of healing. The second was the burden in her life that was weighing heavily on her. I felt that God wanted to encourage her and strengthen her and to heal her pain and set her free from a tormenting weight.

Asking and receiving permission to pray for her, I invited her to take a seat at the table. So as not to draw too much attention to her in the middle of a crowded restaurant, I began to pray with my eyes open just as if we were having a conversation. I asked her to be aware of what was happening in her body as I prayed. "Jesus, thank You that You love Molly. Thank You for Your desire to show her Your love today. I ask in the name of Jesus that You would release Your healing touch into her back. I ask that You would heal her spine from scoliosis and that all the pain associated with this condition would end immediately. I command in the name of Jesus for any troubling and afflicting spirits that have been assigned to cause pain and distress in Molly's life to be gone from her. I pray, Jesus, that You would comfort her and strengthen her in her innermost being to resist the oppression of that which wants to tear her down. In Jesus' name I pray and bless Molly. Amen."

After this brief prayer was over, I asked Molly how she was feeling—if the pain was still there. She circled the table, then lifted her hands and stretched her back and said the pain was gone. When I asked if there was something she couldn't do before I prayed that she could do now, she disappeared to the back of the restaurant for a moment before returning to tell us that she had lifted a heavy tray of plates with no pain in her back. Before we left, I encouraged Molly to consider pursuing afresh a relationship with Jesus that she had started years ago. I also asked her to have her doctor examine her spine, encouraging her with testimonies of people who had a scoliosis diagnosis and who had been healed through prayer.

Caleb heard a word from God, believed in faith that it was from God and was accurate, and then acted on it even though the physical situation of ministering to a waitress in a crowded restaurant at lunchtime was less than ideal. If you are a believer, as you go forth into your daily world, the miraculous gifts of God can follow you so that you, too, can minister to others as Jesus demonstrated in the Gospels. Hearing from God and acting on what we are hearing does not have to be complicated. We are His sheep, His beloved sons and daughters, and He has designed us to hear His voice. We just need to become intimate with God so we can recognize that it is His voice we are hearing, then move with confidence to do what we hear the Father saying. I hope to help you discern the Lord's communications as Eli helped Samuel to recognize he was hearing the audible voice of God. I pray by the end of this book your spirit will be crying out, "Speak, LORD, for your servant is listening" (1 Sam. 3:9).

FOUR

INTIMACY AND FRUITFULNESS

INTIMACY WITH GOD SHOULD BE THE GOAL OF ALL believers. When we live from a place of intimacy as Jesus did, we, too, can hear what the Father is saying and see what the Father is doing, and we can join with Him in the advance of the kingdom.

David Bennett is a student in the Global Awakening Theological Seminary. In addition to being an ordained pastor at Stanwich Congregational Church in Greenwich, Connecticut, David is a private banker at a major bank in the United States where he works with ultra-high-net-worth individuals, hedge funds, asset managers, family offices, and endowments. David has been pastoring on Wall Street for ten years as a marketplace minister, and he has seen God move in mighty ways in the workplace and in his global business travels. He loves to minister to others whenever and wherever he can. Here is one of his testimonies that illustrates the kind of intimacy I am talking about.

While going about my day, I had a vision of someone's right hand, and I saw that their fingers were somewhat closed toward their palm. As I looked at the hand in the vision, I heard the words *carpal tunnel*, relating to numbness and pain from nerve damage. I posted this word of knowledge in the public chat room of the Global Live Online Church as, "carpal tunnel, numbness and pain in hand." A woman named Brenda replied, "Numbness and pain in hand, that's me!" I contacted Brenda by phone and asked her to share with me what was going on and how I could pray for her. She told me she had numbness and pain in her right hand from nerve damage and was worried that she was too old to be healed. She had been suffering with this for many years after working with computers for thirty-five years. All those years of typing had given her carpal tunnel and nerve damage. Then recently she had fallen backward on her right hand while walking her dog. She told me she was basically unable to use her right hand now for much of anything, such as lifting, holding the phone, or washing her hair.

I asked what her pain level was on a scale of zero to ten, zero being no pain and ten being unbearable pain. She said that her pain level was mostly a six to a seven and that the numbness and pain were constant and her hand really hurt. I felt led to cast out her numbness and the pain in her hand and to command the pinched nerves to release. I always look to cast out pain if it exists, but I also had a visual impression to command a release of the pinched nerves. I also felt led to command her hand to be fully healed and fully restored. I asked if she was ready to pray and she said yes. I looked to Jesus and began to pray, "Come, Holy Spirit, upon Brenda and touch her right hand. In the name of Jesus Christ, I rebuke the numbness and pain in your right hand and command the numbness and pain to leave now. In the name of Jesus Christ, I command your pinched nerves to release and to be fully restored. In the name of Jesus Christ, I command your right hand to be fully healed and fully restored." I then declared full healing and full restoration in her right hand and thanked Jesus.

After that prayer, I asked her to move her hand and see if there had been a change in her pain level. Her pain level had gone to a four, and she felt tingling in her body. With her permission, I began to pray again, going for full healing, when I suddenly saw a vision of Jesus kneeling in front of Brenda, smiling as if He was proposing to her. I saw Him grab her right hand in His hand and kiss her hand. I knew I needed to share this vision with her, so I said, "Brenda, Jesus is kissing your hand and saying, 'You are My bride.'" These words just came out of my mouth. The vision was so powerful that it stirred me emotionally and I was caught up in it. Love had entered my soul. Love tender, genuine, and mysterious. I was reveling in the fullness of eternal love.

When I asked her what her pain level was, she said it was gone, praise Jesus! She felt no pain. She then said, "Thank You, Lord, for healing me." I knew I didn't need to pray again. In Mark 11:22, Jesus tells us, "Have faith in God." As a disciple of Jesus, I was seizing the faith of God for Brenda's healing. She was healed. She kept laughing and speaking, but it was hard for me to pay attention to what she was saying because my spirit was still in the vision with Jesus, and I was very emotional. I was in the atmosphere of God, and it was an incredible gift of faith that had a hold on me.

After I got myself together, Brenda and I praised the Lord that she was healed. We both kept laughing with incredible joy. We were experiencing the fullness of joy that exists in God's presence. In Romans 15:13, we read, "May the God of hope fill you with all joy and peace as you trust in him, so that you may overflow with hope by the power of the Holy Spirit." I encouraged Brenda to share her testimony in the Global Live chat room, encouraging her that the power of testimony creates breakthrough, builds faith, and gives glory to God.

I love the intimacy of Jesus in this encounter and the way David was able to see (in a vision) what Jesus was doing and invite Brenda into what Jesus had for her.

LEARNING HIS WAYS

Bill Johnson and I have worked together on a project that addresses the issues of "learning His ways." We ask the questions, "How are we learning God's ways? How is learning His ways causing us to see greater works than we have seen before?" The answers are related to *abiding*—God's words abiding in us as we learn His ways. Knowing how to abide and remain in Him is connected to knowing Him and His ways, and it also comes from knowing His promises (John 14), which gives us an understanding and a basis for our faith. Remember, faith is the condition attached to His promise. We must have faith in Him and His *rhema* words of knowledge or prophecy if we are to do the works He did.

Let's pick up the thread in Scripture that runs from intimacy to fruitfulness. Do you like fruitfulness? I love fruitfulness. In John 15:4–8 Jesus says,

> Remain in me, as I also remain in you. No branch can bear fruit by itself; it must remain in the vine. Neither can you bear fruit unless you remain in me. I am the vine; you are the branches. If you remain in me and I in you, you will bear much fruit; apart from me you can do nothing. If you do not remain in me, you are like a branch that is thrown away and withers; such branches are picked up, thrown into the fire and burned. If you remain in me and my words remain in you, ask whatever you wish, and it will be done for you. This is to my Father's glory, that you bear much fruit, showing yourselves to be my disciples.

Now, this is really interesting. Jesus is saying the revelation that we are His disciples is not only demonstrated by the way we love one another, which you will see in another passage, but this revelation is also demonstrated when we bear fruit for the kingdom. The fruit I am speaking of here is not the fruit of Galatians 5—love, joy, peace, patience, kindness, goodness, faithfulness, gentleness, and self-control. Yes, we should have these fruits. These are the fruits of the Spirit. However, the fruits I am talking about are the fruits that flow from works He says we will do in His name. In the Upper Room Discourse Jesus connects fruitfulness to love and obedience that results in intimacy. This intimacy brings about revelation from the Father and the Son that in turn produces works through faith— faith related to the revelation and works that bring glory to God. All of this comes to the one who abides.

GLORY

In John 15:4–8 Jesus is saying that it is to the Father's glory that we as Christians bear much fruit from the works that can only be accomplished in the power of His Spirit. If we could do them in our flesh, they would not bring glory to God. It is the "Jesus in you"—the Father and Son in you—that is going to enable you to do what you have been given to do, and even greater things because Jesus has gone to the Father. And that is when God receives the glory. There is a commensurate relationship between how much glory is given to God and how much the church, out of obedience and intimacy, receives revelation from God about what He wants us to do. The stronger this relationship, the more we can act in faith and the authority of His name. This is when we begin to see miracles, signs, and wonders take place.

Jesus didn't intend that the Father would be glorified for just the first three hundred years after His crucifixion, until the church was established. Jesus wants the Father to be glorified until He (Jesus) returns. And if the way in which we glorify God is to do those things that cannot be done by our natural ability, then the "gifts" must continue. They are the divine enablements of the Holy Spirit in our lives. Without them we are reduced to what we can accomplish in the natural. We are not to replace the fruits of the Spirit from Galatians 5 with the fruit of John 15. We need both in our lives. It is through both kinds of fruit that God will be glorified. However, in the context of John 15, the deeds are referenced—the "doing" not the "being" of Galatians 5. Jesus said, "If a man remains in me and I in him, he will bear much fruit; apart from me you can *do* nothing." The *doing* here is inclusive of the ministry of healing and deliverance and other acts of mercy and love that bring glory to God. When we talk about intimacy and fruitfulness, both are dependent upon abiding in Christ.

ABIDING

Fruitfulness is related to and dependent upon abiding in Christ (John 15:4). If you stop abiding, start rebelling, stop communing, and become backslidden, you are not going to be very fruitful. You could even say that instead of bringing glory to God, you are bringing shame to His name, because wherever you go and whatever you do after you become His, you join Him to that. That is what Paul said about sexual immorality (1 Cor. 6:12–20). In John 15:5 we see two choices. We can remain (abide) and bear much fruit. Or, if we separate ourselves from Him, we can do nothing. Apart from Him, apart from the anointing of Him in us and through us, we can do nothing. Jesus revisits this connection between revelation and fruitfulness as it pertains to intimacy in verses 15–17, which we will examine later.

HIS WORDS IN US

John 15:7 begins with the word *if*. "If you remain in me and my words remain in you . . ." Why is it important that His words remain in us? Because His words tell us what we can legally ask for; they keep us on track. He is not saying, "You can have an experience with God and never study the Bible." We need to know what the Word says. We need to know who we are in Christ. We also need to know who Christ is in us. If we do not know the Word and do not know our identity in Christ, we are not going to be as fit for the use of the Master as we could be if we know His words.

THE *RHEMA* WORD

"*If* you remain in me and my words remain in you, ask for whatever you wish and it will be done for you" (v. 7, emphasis mine). We have a tendency to read this passage as if it only refers to the Bible. It does refer to the Bible, but it says more than that. It also refers to His freshly spoken *rhema* word. One translation says "Any freshly spoken Rhema word will not be impossible."[1] Remember, a *rhema* word is a word from heaven, through an individual, about something they are to do, which carries with it the power of God to bring the word given into reality. There is a condition here though. A *rhema* word needs faith in order to become reality—*if* faith rises in the person because of their understanding of this rhema/word/communication.

As Paul said in 2 Corinthians 4:13, "It is written: 'I believed; therefore I have spoken.' Since we have that same spirit of faith, we also believe and therefore speak." It is the *revelation* that causes faith. This is where God in His sovereignty chose to include us in some of His works. The *rhema* word is a sovereign moment in which God wants to do something through us and for someone else, though it could also be through us for us. Here is another testimony from Brian Starley, whose experience with the motorcycle club members you read earlier. It illustrates a *rhema* word that brought healing and freedom.

I was with my wife in a distant city, preaching and ministering at a conference. During our third night there, I had a word of knowledge for a woman dealing with severe stomach pain and frequent nausea. I knew that this pain and sickness had something to do with the number four. I also knew there was a connection with the number thirty-three. This word of knowledge came in three parts by two different means of revelation. The first thing that happened was seeing a mental picture of a woman holding her stomach and bent over in a lot of pain and uneasiness. Second, I heard a brief impression of the number four. Last, I had an image of the number thirty-three.

While I was confident in the accuracy of the word of knowledge, I was not given any additional insight into the interpretation. So rather than explaining what I thought the stomach issue and numbers were, I just gave the word. As soon as I finished delivering the word of knowledge, a woman seated in the back stood and waved that it was her. After the service, the woman came up and I was able to pray for her.

She first told me that everything I said applied to her and went on to explain how. She said, "For the past four years, I've been dealing with excruciating stomach pain. It has been nearly 24/7, and I am so miserable. I'm also thirty-three years old. When you said those things, I knew that you were talking about me!" I then began encouraging her before continuing the interview. I said, "That's amazing. I don't know if you were here for the teaching earlier today, but we talked about what words of knowledge mean. One of those meanings is that God deeply knows us. I believe that He gave me this word for you to let you know that He sees you and wants to heal you." She was very thankful for the reminder. I continued by asking, "Have you visited a doctor or gotten a diagnosis for what is wrong with your stomach?"

She responded, "Yes, and no. I have gone several times to different doctors, and while I've been medicated for various symptoms, there has been no official diagnosis. Some have even said that nothing is wrong with me, or that it's in my head. But that isn't the case. The pain has been intense and persistent since it began."

This was unusual and prompted me to ask about her life surrounding when the problem started. I did this because we know that certain events can create trauma and lead to physical symptoms. I said, "You said that this started very suddenly about four years ago, correct? Can you tell me if anything significant took place in your life during that time? Was there anything that could have caused it outright in the natural, or perhaps a traumatic event?"

After asking this, she began to look very upset and worried and then started weeping. Soon after, she began explaining to me that she had only recently started getting involved in this church. Prior to that she was involved in the occult. She did not go into detail about her conversion but said to me that immediately afterward, she knew she needed to leave the occult group. She cut all ties with them and began following the Lord. When I asked what year she left, she said it was 2016.

I knew when she told me this that there was a connection between the year she left and the beginning of her pain. Before I could ask any other questions, the Holy Spirit spoke to me and said, *She was cursed by the other members of the group when she left.* Rather than addressing the symptoms, I thought it best to deal with the root cause and prayed a commanding prayer, breaking the curse off of her life.

I first shared with her the connection between her illness and the occult group she was formerly involved with. I then told her that I would begin praying for the curse to be broken. After placing my hand on her shoulder, I prayed, "Holy

Spirit, come and let Your presence rest on us." After waiting for a short time, I said, "In the name of Jesus, I come against the curse spoken over you. I command it to be broken. I command every effect of witchcraft to leave your body right now." After only a few seconds of praying this, she began shaking and fell to the floor unconscious. I believe that this was a combination of God's power touching her and the Enemy's power departing. She was on the floor, shaking and nonresponsive for fifteen minutes, and then she woke up.

I helped her up and over to a chair. Before I could ask anything further, she began crying again, this time joyfully. She said, "There is no more pain in my stomach! It's all gone! Thank You, Jesus!" I rejoiced with her for the healing that took place. I then remembered a critical piece that I had forgotten to ask earlier. I said, "I know you gave your life to Jesus, but did anyone ever lead you through repentance of the involvement in the occult?" She said that someone did at another church, and I asked if we could do that one more time. I did this because I was not familiar with the other person or their way of doing things, and I wanted to be sure it was done correctly.

She agreed, and we prayed together. I led her in a prayer renouncing her involvement in the occult and repenting for worshiping idols. I then asked if she had any items from her time with the group, and she said that she didn't. I believe in asking these questions and renouncing involvement to sever any remaining ties with the Enemy. After we prayed together, I encouraged her to keep thanking God for what He had done in her. I then said that she should continue attending church, specifically the church where we were right then. I did this since I know their leadership and the spiritual health of the congregation. Additionally, I emphasized the importance of abiding in Christ and avoiding any possible temptation to return to former paths. I recommended several books for her to continue growing in the Lord and studying the topic of deliverance. I told her that God could use her to bring similar breakthroughs to others and told her of her testimony's power.

If we have Christ's words from Scripture abiding in us, if we have His *rhema* revelatory word that comes to us from the Spirit, it will create great faith to speak out. John 15:7 says, "If you abide in Me, and My words abide in you, you will ask what you desire, and it shall be done for you" (NKJV). The "if" and the "and" indicate a double condition that involves remaining in Christ and His words remaining in us. This is very important; it is an emphasis from the school of the Word of Faith stream of teaching, which they have drawn from Jesus—knowing how to abide and to remain in Him is connected to knowing His will and His ways. Moses said, "Show me your ways" (Ex. 33:13, paraphrase). My exhortation to you, the reader, is to cry out to God for Him to show you His power, and more importantly, for God to show you His ways. In learning the ways of God, we learn better how to cooperate with God. And, when we cooperate with God, we see the power of God. You cannot obey a command or communique that you didn't perceive or understand. It is in the place of intimacy that we learn to better hear our Shepherd's voice. In order to obey specific commands from God, we need to learn the ways of God—how the Holy Spirit operates.

Obedience to God's commands is critical not only for intimacy with Him but also for the fruit of healing and miracles to occur in the lives of Jesus' followers. This obedience is not to be limited to the moral commands of Scripture, but also to the commands to do things "prompted by faith" and "working through love" that are the keys to experiencing the power of God (2 Thess. 1:11; Gal. 5:5 ESV). God's power for supernatural expressions of His grace comes from working to bring good news to the poor, heal, set the captives free (deliverance); binding up the brokenhearted (emotional or inner healing); bringing the wisdom of God to society's problems (addressing the powers and authorities); and breaking down the gates of hell (entering the strong man's house that Jesus bound and plundering his goods).[2]

"AND THE GREATEST OF THESE IS LOVE"

I want to look briefly now at the relationship between revelation and fruitfulness as it pertains to intimacy with Christ as found in John 15:15–17.

I no longer call you servants, because a servant does not know his master's business. Instead, I have called you friends, for everything that I learned from my Father I have made known to you. You did not choose me, but I chose you and appointed you so that you might go and bear fruit—fruit that will last—and so that whatever you ask in my name the Father will give you. This is my command: Love each other.

You see, He did not save us just to get us to heaven. As a matter of fact, He did not say, "I chose you so that you could go to heaven." We get to go to heaven as a side benefit of Jesus' finished work on

49

the cross. The primary reason that Jesus chose us (and the Father told Him who to choose) is so we can bear much fruit.

In America we tend to want a formula, something we can grab hold of. We forget all about bearing fruit and abiding and listening. We forget about receiving the revelation. Reliance on a formalistic method of connecting with God that strictly adheres to rules and tradition can cause one to forget about and ultimately miss opportunities to abide and listen for His voice. It is in that place of abiding and listening that revelation can come. But I want to tell you this secret. Simply ask in His name, and then in obedience follow the revelation He gives you. By embracing the great command to love one another as Christ loves us, we will create the atmosphere in which these things can take place, because these gifts will have no value if they are not motivated by love (1 Cor. 13; Col. 1:12–13).

We must be careful not to misread 1 Corinthians 13:1-13, the great "love chapter," and think love is better than the gifts or that fruit is better than the gifts. Remember, 1 Corinthians 13 is preceded by 1 Corinthians 12, which teaches about the spiritual gifts and ends with "but earnestly desire the higher gifts" (v. 31 ESV). Then, chapter 14 tells us to earnestly desire the spiritual gifts, especially the gift of prophecy (v. 1). God is saying in these chapters that we must understand that the motivation for exercising the gifts needs to come from His love. His love is both a fruit and a gift rooted in the grace of God—a love that grows through our intimacy with Jesus. We are planted in Jesus. He is the soil; we are the seed. Abiding and obedience waters the seed in the soil, causing our deeds to be motivated by love and prompted by faith.

Jesus talks about "going" in Matthew 28:19–20: "Therefore go and make disciples of all nations, baptizing them in the name of the Father and of the Son and of the Holy Spirit, and teaching them to obey everything I have commanded you." Sadly, the church has appropriated this command "go" from Jesus as if it were another moral command, in essence a part of the Ten Commandments. While we certainly ought to obey the Ten Commandments and the other moral commandments found in Scripture, do we have to totally ignore what Jesus was really saying in Matthew 10:7–8: "As you go, proclaim this message: 'The kingdom of heaven has come near.' Heal the sick, raise the dead, cleanse those who have leprosy, drive out demons"? What Jesus is saying in Matthew 28:20 when He says, "teaching them to obey everything I have commanded you," is that we are to heal the sick, raise the dead, cleanse the lepers, cast out demons, and bring good news to the poor.

The following story is from one of my former interns, Will Hart, who is currently a Global Awakening Theological Seminary student taking the physical healing class. Will is CEO of Iris Global, a mission movement serving the poor with a focus on the Beatitudes. Iris Global, provides both humanitarian aid and spiritual aid through the gospel of Jesus Christ in Africa, Asia, Europe, the Middle East, and the Americas, with sixty-five bases worldwide in thirty-four nations. In his late teens, Will was radically saved by God and immediately began moving in the supernatural. Since that time, Will has traveled the world, ministering wherever God leads him. God is using Will in ways large and small as he answers Jesus' call in Matthew 10:7.

My first word of knowledge and first healing some twenty years ago changed my life profoundly in a moment. Since that time, the word of knowledge gift has grown to become my most frequently used gift of the Spirit. It happened in December 1999, when I attended my first-ever spirit-filled conference. I was saved only two months prior during a small gathering where the Holy Spirit overwhelmed me. Fully yielding my life to Him, I became so hungry to grow in the gifts of the Spirit. I was seventeen years old at the time, and began fasting and praying for more of God. A friend told me about this event on the other side of my state. I drove out to the conference without even registering. It was a four-hour drive from my house, and I had nowhere to sleep. God provided a way, and I ended up sleeping on the floor of an attendee's hotel room. I was hungry for more. I had become wonderfully passionate for the kingdom and His presence, and nothing was going to stop me.

On the second day of a three-day conference, I walked into Dr. Randy Clark's session on words of knowledge. A young man named Ben was traveling with Randy, and Ben and Randy shared the session. At the end of their session, Dr. Clark prayed for everyone to receive an impartation. I closed my eyes and cried out for God to give me words of knowledge. I felt nothing—no power, no heat, no physical manifestation. Frustrated, I opened my eyes and saw many people had raised their hands as a sign that God had given them a word. I immediately thought this gift must not be for me. As soon as that thought passed through my head, the words NERVOUS SCIATICA floated in front of my eyes. This was my first and, to this day, the clearest example of "reading" a word of knowledge I have ever received. The words started in my right eye, floating to the left, exactly like a news ticker on your television.

My first thought was, *Was that me?* Immediately I thought that I had made it up out of my emotion. Dr. Clark teaches that we are to resist the thought that a word we have received is not important or that it is "just you." We must remember that it builds faith in the other person to know that God has revealed their condition to you. What seems like a vague impression to you may be a shout to the other person! As this inner struggle took place, I found some peace in the fact that I had no idea what nervous sciatica was. When the call went out for those who were skeptical that they really had a word of knowledge to come forward, I approached the platform for the first time in my life. Fear and uncertainty overwhelmed each thought as Dr. Clark started at the front of the line and worked his way toward me. After a few minutes, it was my turn. I cautiously fumbled over my words as I told the attendees the words I saw float across my eyes. As the words *nervous sciatica* left my mouth, I heard a scream from the auditorium's far left side. A woman jumped up and screamed, "That's me!" Within moments, she had made her way up front ready to be healed. I will refer to this woman as Grace.

I remember her faith was over the top. She kept on repeating, "I knew this was going to happen. I knew it." Within another minute or two, three other women came up and joined Grace in response to the word. My first question to Grace was, "What is a nervous sciatica?" All four women turned to their side, pointing to the nerve that runs from the hip down the leg. Each one had a different problem with her sciatic nerve.

I found out later that sciatic nerve issues are wide ranging. Some issues go away within days; others can go on for years and can be so painful they can lead to loss of bowel control. Grace had been in pain for thirteen years; another woman for eight years. The other two women never explained how long; they just said they wanted healing. This was one of my first times praying for sick people. To say I was nervous would be a complete understatement.

Grace's faith was overwhelmingly high; she had been asking God for this moment for a long time. I barely laid hands on her as she fell to the floor. I remember saying, "Be healed in Jesus' name," as she fell under the Spirit's power. Two things immediately took place in my heart. The first was faith, and the second was boldness. Watching Jesus move so quickly through my hands and prayers was life changing. As the three other women observed what happened to the first, tangible faith flooded all of us. I prayed the simple commanding prayer, "Be healed in Jesus name," and within moments all four were on the floor. I just stood there, laughing nervously at what had just happened. I was shocked at what took place, even before I heard the testimonies.

I was able to interview Grace the next morning. I remember walking into the dining area and seeing her sitting with her husband. I asked her if she still had any pain, and she told me this was the first time in thirteen years she woke up painless. Jesus sent out the seventy-two, and the Bible says they came back rejoicing, shocked that the demons departed as they called on the name of Jesus (Luke 10:1–17). As I write this, I can still feel that moment of rejoicing, the awe that Jesus chose to use me, a broken vessel. To the best of my recollection, Grace's healing is the first miracle I witnessed when I physically prayed for someone. Most importantly, this moment started a chain of events that has led me to sit with everyone from billionaires to the poorest of the poor, moving in the gift of word of knowledge. The same words flow just as they did at that first encounter with Dr. Randy, when the Holy Spirit deposited a most cherished gift of grace in me.

"TO LEAVEN THE WHOLE WORLD"

When we bear fruit, we reveal we are truly Christ's disciples. This is simple, but what does it say for church life when this is not happening? When the Christian life has been reduced to just good morals, it does not bring the fullest amount of glory to the Father. It is not the fullness of life that God intends for us. My desire for spiritual gifts and the power and authority of the Holy Spirit is not so that I can have "a good feeling." It is so that my life will bring glory, the proper kind of glory, to the Father.

When I was pastoring a church, which I did for thirty years of my now fifty years of ministry, my desire was that we would be a church that brought glory to the Father, not just on Sundays through the worship, but every day in every way by hearing what He said to us, stepping out with what we heard, and believing that He wanted to use us as salt and light. I believe that God wants not only to transform those within the church but also desires that we, the church, then take that same leaven, that same transformative power that comes from God, and sow it into the world (Matt. 28:16–20).

AUTHORITY AND POWER,
PRESENCE AND JOY

Within the final message Jesus told His disciples before His death was a message of joy. He knew they would be facing a time of almost unbearable grief upon His crucifixion, and He wanted them to understand the joy that would be theirs—and ours.

We know that Jesus is the vine and we are the branches who must "abide" in Him if we are to be the church in the world. Apart from Jesus we have no source of life or fruitfulness. *Meno*, the Greek concept for the word *abide*, is a verb that means "to remain, to stay, to lodge, or encamp." There is a relationship between abiding in Jesus and joy, yet sadly the church often seems to find more comfort in sadness than in joy. We have become comfortable with grief and godly sorrow, but we seem to find it hard to move past the godly sorrow into the joy of the Lord. You might say that crying is to sadness as laughter is to joy. Joy is an important biblical concept. Jesus said,

> As the Father has loved me, so have I loved you. Now remain in
> my love. If you keep my commands, you will remain in my love,
> just as I have kept my Father's commands and remain in his love.
> I have told you this so that my joy may be in you and that your
> joy may be complete. My command is this: Love each other as I
> have loved you. (John 15:9–12)

These are indeed powerful words, yet we seem to have trouble with the "joy" part. I have heard people essentially say, "God doesn't want you to have joy. God doesn't want you to have fun. Church should not be fun. There shouldn't be so much joy in church. You need to be sorry for your sins, you worm." This is not what Scripture says. It says, "There is a time for everything, and a season for every activity under the heavens . . . a time to weep and a time to laugh, a time to mourn and a time to dance" (Eccl. 3:1, 4). My reply to those people is, "I came to the cross and my worm got nailed to the cross. I am not the worm anymore. I am in Christ. I am seated with Him in heavenly places. My old self died on the cross. I am now raised with Christ. I am the beloved. I am the apple of His eye. I live with a sense of the authority and pleasure of God that enables me to come boldly to the throne of grace that I might find help in my time of need."

I have moved from the kingdom of darkness to the kingdom of light. My identity is now not a sinner, but a saint. I have been teaching and ministering all over the world, with miracles, signs, and wonders following, for twenty-six years now—and teaching others how to receive communications from God that lead to faith for healing for thirty-seven years. It never gets old. I never grow tired of seeing people healed, delivered, and set free in the power of the cross of Jesus Christ. It brings me great joy to see others' joy and to know that it is all for the glory of God. My first fourteen years of ministry—when I had not yet begun to understand how to hear from God or see His power to heal—were not nearly so full of joy. During those years I saw about five people healed. I thank God every day for answering my prayer in 1971 to empower me to live the fullness of the Christian life, hearing from God and being used supernaturally to advance His kingdom.

Jesus gives us these truths in the Upper Room Discourse so we are able to have joy in us, and so that our joy may be complete. At least that is part of the reason for the discourse. Jesus essentially said, "I want you to have so much joy, so I am going to tell you the secrets of My joy: Do not rebel against Me. Do you want to have joy? Do not give yourself to sin. Do you want to have joy? Stay out of shame. Do you want to have joy? Obey Me. Do you want to have joy? Let Me abide in you. When you are obedient to Me, and when you love one another as I have loved you, I will abide in you."

You see, Jesus has a joy for us that can't be taken away. It is a joy that springs from authority, an authority given to us to ask and receive. In the finished work of the cross we can ask the Father for anything in the name of His Son, Jesus. Jesus told us about this joy:

> So with you: Now is your time of grief, but I will see you again and you will rejoice, and no one will take away your joy. In that day you will no longer ask me anything. Very truly I tell you, my Father will give you whatever you ask in my name. Until now you have not asked for anything in my name. Ask and you will receive, and your joy will be complete. (John 16:22–24)

Having studied Jesus' instructions in John's gospel from the Upper Room Discourse, let's trace the thread through seven key insights:

1. The Father receives glory through works done by the followers of Jesus in Jesus' name. (John 14:10–14)
2. Intimacy with Jesus and revelation through the Holy Spirit are related, and this intimacy is related to obedience. (John 14:15–22)
3. Intimacy is important to bearing fruit—the fruit of doing as well as the fruit of being. (John 15:4–8)

4. Intimacy produces friendship with Jesus and is dependent upon obedience to what He commands. This results in revelation from the Father, through the Son, by the Holy Spirit. This revelation creates the knowledge to know what to ask in His will and to ask it in faith. (John 15:12–17)

5. The revelation from the Spirit of truth that comes out of intimacy is the basis for Jesus' followers to bring glory to Him. (John 16:12–15)

6. Abiding in Jesus, remaining in His love, is related to obedience to His commands, which results in Jesus' joy being in His followers and His disciples—their joy being complete. (John 15:9–11)

7. Out of this relationship of intimacy with Jesus, we are to ask in order to receive, and our joy will be complete. (John 16:22–24)

Now that we have a better understanding of what it means to minister out of a place of intimacy with Jesus, I want us to follow the thread that connects obedience that flows from intimacy to the role of that intimate obedience in the ministry of healing as found in the gospel of John.

FIVE

UNDERSTANDING OBEDIENCE

I BELIEVE THERE IS A PRINCIPLE THAT THE HOLY Spirit wants us to understand if we are to experience the extravagance of God through the miraculous. It all starts with learning to "do whatever he tells you" (John 2:5). The miracles of God that we find in the Scriptures, particularly in the gospel of John, are typically preceded by a request from God. These requests are His points of contact for a release of faith, because faith needs to have an element of risk for it to be faith. I believe that God delights in the kind of faith that leads to obedience. God wants us to stretch our faith in the midst of risk and experience His extravagant love for us. If we will just take Him at His word, focusing on His invitation rather than our problems, we will see a release of the miraculous that will bring great glory to God.

I am using the term *word* here in the sense of hearing the instructions of God for what He wants to do. These instructions could be in the form of a prophecy or a word of knowledge. It is important to make the distinction between God's promises and His *rhema* word. The promises of the Bible are helpful in understanding general principles of God, whereas a *rhema* word gives direction in specific situations. It is important to note that this is not raising subjectivity above the objectivity of the Word of God—the Bible; rather, objective biblical instruction and narratives point us to the reality of God's Spirit communicating with humans on the subjective level of impressions, feelings, visions, dreams, and understanding the providential moments when we realize we are in a divine appointment where God has orchestrated events for His purposes.

In the gospel of John there are seven miracles—seven supernatural events—recorded. Seven is the number of fullness. The apostle John had some of the greatest insights into the ministry of Jesus in all of Scripture. He recorded things that are not found in the Synoptic Gospels. There is a reason and significance for every detail John has included in his gospel. Led by the Spirit, he selectively chose the miracles that we find in the book of John, and it is interesting to note that every one of these supernatural events is preceded by a request from Jesus, asking the people who are going to experience the miracles to do something first.

"DO WHATEVER HE TELLS YOU"

We start with John's presentation of the miracle at Cana.

> On the third day a wedding took place at Cana in Galilee. Jesus' mother was there, and Jesus and his disciples had also been invited to the wedding. When the wine was gone, Jesus' mother said to him, "They have no more wine." "Woman, why do you involve me?" Jesus replied. "My hour has not yet come." His mother said to the servants, "Do whatever he tells you." (John 2:1–5)

Jesus' mother's directive to the servants in this passage—"Do whatever he tells you"—is one of the most profound insights in Scripture regarding breakthrough in the supernatural. This is what our response to Jesus needs to be—to do whatever He says.

> Nearby stood six stone water jars, the kind used by the Jews for ceremonial washing, each holding from twenty to thirty gallons.
>
> Jesus said to the servants, "Fill the jars with water"; so they filled them to the brim. (vv. 6–7)

EXTRAVAGANT OBEDIENCE

I want to stop here for a moment because this detail is important. The servants filled the jars to the brim. The servants were extravagant in their obedience. I know this from my own experience. I used to carry water to the horses and the cows on our farm. I had to fill up two five-gallon buckets of water and carry them from the pond down to the place where some of the horses were stalled. I never filled them to the brim because if I did they would spill down my legs. I would get all wet and would not have nearly as much water in the buckets when I arrived at the barn. So I would fill them up only to a certain point so they would not spill as I carried them. John is telling us that the servants filled the stone water jars to the brim. This is an extravagant response to Jesus' instruction representative of complete obedience.

> Then he told them, "Now draw some out and take it to the master of the banquet." They did so, and the master of the banquet tasted the water that had been turned into wine. He did not realize where it came from, though the servants who had drawn the water knew. (vv. 8–9)

RESPONDING IN FAITH

From this passage it is not clear when the water turned to wine, but I think it is an important aspect of the story to examine. There are two possibilities. Either the water turned into wine when the servants drew it and poured it into the pots, or it turned into wine after they drew it out of the pots and were taking it to the master of the banquet. If that's the case, then on the way to the master of the banquet, they were carrying water, knowing that he wanted wine. I think this is when the water turned into wine.

"Jesus said to the servants, 'Fill the jars with water'"(v. 7). The servants did not draw wine; they drew water, and that, I think, is the key. The servants acted in faith. They had drawn water, they knew it, and somehow, by the time they got to the master of the banquet, the water had turned into wine. I believe that God delights in faith. He delights in obedience, even when it seems that we are doing something foolish. There is something about God telling us to do something that does not make sense in the natural that pulls on our faith.

Take the story in Matthew 17, for example. Tax collectors approached the disciple Peter and asked if Jesus intended to pay the temple tax. Knowing they had no money, Peter asked Jesus what they were to do, and Jesus replied, "But so that we may not cause offense, go to the lake and throw out your line. Take the first fish you catch; open its mouth and you will find a four-drachma coin. Take it and give it to them for my tax and yours" (v. 27). Finding the coins you need to pay your taxes in the mouth of a fish that you just pulled out of the water makes no sense in the natural. Yet, in faith Peter was obedient, and the result of his obedience was the miraculous.

The kind of faith we see in the Gospels that accompanies

miracles, signs, and wonders can be seen today. My friends Heidi and Rolland Baker operate daily in this kind of faith and see much fruit. Here is my rendering of one of their testimonies as told by Heidi to me.

When Heidi flew into England, a paraplegic man in a wheelchair was there to pick her up (his wife had driven). This man had been prayed for thousands of times, and he kept track of all those prayers in a journal. Heidi thought to herself, *God, You have to heal him!* She heard the Lord say to her, *I'm going to heal him on Saturday* (it was Thursday), but she did not tell the man. This man had no movement in his legs; he had a severed spine and suffered from multiple sclerosis.

Saturday came and Heidi knew that the man was going to be healed. As Heidi and Rolland were praying for him, he first began to get movement in his hand, which was originally hindered because of his MS. One side of this man's body started shaking, and he yelled, "It's hot! It's hot!" He had a severed spine so he could not feel anything before this. So they picked him up from his wheelchair, and the Lord spoke to Heidi, telling her to "kick the man's leg." At this point, only one side of this man's body was healed, so they gently kicked the man's leg on the side that was not healed. They kept moving around his body gently kicking this man's other leg. Each time they did this, Heidi said he would get stronger and his leg would shake and he would feel "power/fire in it," and it would move. They did this for about a half hour and then the man started walking on his own. His wife and children were weeping along with Heidi and Rolland as they watched our glorious Lord heal this man. Like Heidi, this man personally heard from God that he was going to be healed on Saturday, but neither he nor Heidi knew the other had heard this from God. Heidi said that it was his faith, Heidi's faith, and Rolland's faith that all came together. This man was so thoroughly healed that he began leaping and jumping and dancing.

GLORY, POWER, AND THE MIRACULOUS

As we read the remainder of this passage in John, we are given the first revelation of Jesus' glory through the miracles He performed.

> Then he [the master of the banquet] called the bridegroom aside and said, "Everyone brings out the choice wine first and then the cheaper wine after the guests have had too much to drink; but you have saved the best till now." What Jesus did here in Cana of Galilee was the first of the signs through *which he revealed his glory; and his disciples believed in him*. (John 2:9–11, emphasis mine)

How did He reveal His glory? By the miracle, by the demonstration of power; and that is an important way His glory is revealed today. That is also the main way God revealed His glory in the history of His chosen people, recorded in the Bible.

The apostles John and Paul understood this connection between glory and power. Paul used *glory* and *power* as synonyms. "The body that is sown is perishable, it is raised imperishable; it is sown in dishonor, it is raised in glory; it is sown in weakness, it is raised in power" (1 Cor. 15:42–43).

Paul also wrote, "Just as Christ was raised from the dead through the *glory* of the Father" (Rom. 6:4, emphasis mine). And, as already mentioned, John wrote, "What Jesus did here in Cana of Galilee was the first of the signs through which he revealed his glory; and his disciples believed in him." This verse makes the connection between God's glory and His miraculous works, and it also illustrates the element of faith—faith that came about as a result of the miraculous work of Jesus.

A number of years ago I was at Bill Johnson's church. I was getting ready to preach for the first time this message on the connection between glory and power and the miraculous, using seven signs from Scripture to illustrate my points. I heard the Lord say to me, *I don't want you to just teach this message. I want you to model it.* This was followed by the clear impression that God wanted to heal digestive problems. So I said, "I think God is going to heal us of anything wrong with our digestion; anything from the mouth through the whole system." I felt like there would be about fifteen to twenty people who would come forward in response to this word of knowledge.

Then I said, "This is what I think we are supposed to do: any of you who have anything wrong with your digestive system come up to the front." Two hundred people came forward! As I spoke, I not only received the impression of healing for digestive issues, but I had a mental picture of people standing and bending at the waist backward and forward. I believed this was the act of obedience God wanted us to do as a point of contact to release faith. I asked the Lord, "How long are we to do this?" I didn't get an answer so I chose two minutes. Realizing that what I had just asked them to do could end up being awkward (you don't want to bend forward and have your head or nose touching the person's butt in front of you), I needed to apply 1 Corinthians 14:40, "But all things should be done decently and in order" (ESV). I lined up the people in two rows across the front of the room, with about seven feet between each line. The bending backward and forward made no sense in the natural, but it was the impression from the Holy Spirit—at least I thought it was—and there was no way of knowing if I was really hearing correctly other than to do what God said and see if healings occurred.

For two minutes we stood in place, leaning back far and then leaning forward to about a ninety-degree angle. I knew that we needed to do this long enough to begin to feel foolish, but not so long that we passed out. Then I released them to go back to their seats, explaining that many would not know if they were healed until some time had passed—until they ate something—because that is how it is with digestive issues. I remember thinking, *If a visitor came into the church at this moment and saw two hundred people bobbing back and forward at the waist, lined up at the front of the pulpit, the visitor would think we had lost our minds.* All this happened at the beginning of the sermon as I began teaching on faith, the first of the seven signs in Scripture that illustrate the connection between glory, power, and the miraculous. Of the seven signs, this was the only one I didn't have an illustration for, so God illustrated it for me by this act of obedience. I had to act on faith, in a split second, in response to what I thought I was hearing.

No one there that night knew, but I was experiencing digestive problems myself. My grandfather had died of colon cancer, and for the past two months I had been losing blood when I went to the bathroom. I was very concerned but scared to go to the doctor. I was believing for a miracle of healing for myself that night, and I got one! I was healed. Faith combined with obedience released the miraculous.

During the next few days I heard many, many testimonies of healing in response to that initial act of obedience on my part and the obedience of those who came forward and spent two minutes bending forward and backward. They knew they could keep their anonymity if they told the church receptionist over the phone, and that helped people to share their testimonies. One woman who had a bad case of hemorrhoids for more than fifty years woke up healed the next day. Allergies to foods were healed. Many kinds of colon or small intestine problems were healed. Many kinds of stomach problems were healed. Mouth problems and esophagus problems were healed. God received much glory through the acts of obedience and faith.

FOCUS ON THE INVITATION

Often we can get so caught up focusing on our problems that we miss Jesus' invitation. When we take Jesus at His word, focusing on His invitation rather than our problems, we will see the glory of God in a release of the miraculous. This truth is demonstrated in John 4 when Jesus healed the official's son. In this story we find Jesus in Cana of Galilee again.

> Once more he visited Cana in Galilee, where he had turned the water into wine. And there was a certain royal official whose son lay sick at Capernaum. When this man heard that Jesus had arrived in Galilee from Judea, he went to him *and begged him to come and heal his son*, who was close to death.
>
> "Unless you people see signs and wonders," Jesus told him, "you will never believe."

The royal official said, *"Sir, come down before my child dies."*

"Go," Jesus replied, "your son will live."

The man took Jesus at his word and departed. While he was still on the way, his servants met him with the news that his boy was living. When he inquired as to the time when his son got better, they said to him, "Yesterday, at one in the afternoon, the fever left him."

Then the father realized that this was the exact time at which Jesus had said to him, "Your son will live." *So he and his whole household believed.*

This was the second sign Jesus performed after coming from Judea to Galilee. (John 4:46–54, emphasis mine)

I want to stop for a moment and look at Jesus' first response to the royal official's request to heal his son. Jesus said, "Unless you people see miraculous signs and wonders . . . you will never believe." Most commentators I have read interpret this as Jesus putting a negative value on faith related to signs and wonders. Some commentators refer to it as "signs faith," a secondary faith that is not as good as the faith one has without seeing signs and wonders. I disagree with this interpretation.

This interpretation essentially says that great faith does not need miracles. This viewpoint would interpret Jesus' response with a negative inflection, almost with condemnation. "Unless you people see miracles, miraculous signs and wonders, you will never believe." (Read with a gruff, stern inflection.) Then there is another interpretation, without negative inflection or a tone of condemnation, without gruffness. Try reading the same words with compassion (Jesus healed out of compassion) and an understanding of the importance of signs to faith. When you do, you find an honest recognition of the importance of signs and wonders: "Unless you people see miraculous signs and wonders, you are not going to believe." This slight change in inflection makes a difference in interpretation, and brings us to that place of belief that Jesus understood.

Unfortunately, many of us have been taught to interpret this statement with a negative connotation, creating a negative view of the relationship between signs and wonders and faith. Paul wrote to the church in Corinth, "*Jews demand signs* and Greeks look for wisdom" (1 Cor. 1:22, emphasis mine). This indicates how common knowledge connected the need for Jews to have signs to believe. Jesus would have been aware of this reality and accommodated them in His humility.

TAKE JESUS AT HIS WORD

Now let's examine the royal official's reply to Jesus. The royal official said, "Sir, come down before my child dies." This man's statement indicates that he knew who Jesus was. He had heard about Jesus, and he knew that when Jesus laid hands on the sick, they recovered. He knew that Jesus trained His disciples to lay hands on the sick. Perhaps he had heard about the woman with the issue of blood who was healed when she touched the edge of Jesus' cloak (Luke 8:43–48). Or perhaps he heard about how Jesus healed Peter's mother-in-law with a touch (Matt. 8:14–15). There is an emphasis in Scripture on the glory and the power of God moving from Jesus' body to those who touch Him or whom He touches.[1] This royal official had an understanding of the significance and importance of Jesus laying His hands on people. He understood the power that comes from a touch from Jesus. For this reason, he was anxious for

Jesus to come to his house and lay hands on his son who was dying. In the short description of his dialogue with Jesus, he asks Jesus twice to come to his house (vv. 47, 49).

Watch what Jesus said in response to this father. "Jesus replied, 'You may go. Your son will live.' The man took Jesus at his word and departed." There it is; that is the key—*the man took Jesus at His word*, and because he took Jesus at His word, his son was healed. If you read this in context, the man asked Jesus to come to his house more than once, and Jesus' response was, "Go." Therefore, this father just believed what Jesus said and went home. He reached out and grabbed hold of the raw word of God. His obedience was an indication that he did believe Jesus' words, "You may go. Your son will live." The royal official's act of obedience was an indication of his faith. His son was healed!

STEP OUT IN FAITH

A number of years ago I was in a meeting in the Dominican Republic and I felt like the Lord said, *Sing a song.* It wasn't just any song. Through an impression, He gave me a particular song that we were to sing and told me that when we sang it He would heal many of the people there. I heard Him say, *Just have them sing the song, count to three and give a shout, and I will heal them.* Since that time, out of the hundreds and hundreds of meetings I have conducted, I have heard God ask that of me maybe less than twenty times. But when He asked me that first time in the Dominican Republic, I confess that I was scared to do it. I thought, *God, what if it doesn't work? Is this You or is it just me?*

It is so much easier to follow the leadings of the Lord when we hear an audible voice or have an open vision rather than a split-second impression or a fleeting mental picture. All I had that night was a split-second impression with a mental picture that we were to sing this song and God would heal the people. I am here to tell you that it takes more faith to declare a fleeting impression than it does the audible voice of God or a vision from God. I think He sometimes speaks to us in fleeting impressions because He is pleased by our faith when we respond in obedience. When I stepped out in faith that night, hundreds of people received healings.

Let me put this in context. At the start of the conference, I had asked my host how much time I would have to preach. He told me just to do whatever the Lord led me to do and that I could have all the time I wanted. The night before, I had taken a long time to explain words of knowledge, then I had given words of knowledge. Then we prayed for the sick. All this was being translated from English into Spanish. There had not been time for a sermon because I was going for healing. The next day I had an impression that I was to preach a sermon in the night service. It was going to be important to preach a certain sermon to the people.

The hosting apostle told me again to preach as long as I wanted, as the Lord led. However, just before 10:00 p.m., nearly 60 percent of the people got up and left the tent (there were about twenty-five hundred people in the tent). I asked the pastor what happened that so many left all at once. He told me that those people came by bus and the last bus was at ten.

Realizing now that 60 percent of the people had to leave to catch the bus by ten, I knew there wouldn't be time to preach an entire message—in two languages, after a long worship time—and have time for words of knowledge and prayer for healing. During worship, the anointing increased when one particular song was sung. That is when I had the impression about God healing if we would sing that song again. During worship, He reminded me how years before He had awakened me with one of the two or three strongest impressions I have ever had from God. The impression was, *I want you to realize that when My presence is in your midst in worship, so is My power to heal!*

There is something about not speaking in your own church that gives freedom to step out in faith. When you speak away from home, you know that if you are wrong in what you say and do, you never have to return and face that crowd of people again. This realization has helped me step out and test whether or not I am hearing from God, which in turn has created new levels of faith in me to "go for it." When I do and experience a breakthrough, I take that back to my own church and my own ministry. When I am accurately hearing from God and acting on what I hear, the fruit of my actions causes faith to rise in the hearts of the audience.

ACCEPT THE INVITATION

Let's examine a third miracle that is found in the gospel of John.

> Some time later, Jesus went up to Jerusalem for one of the Jewish festivals. Now there is in Jerusalem near the Sheep Gate a pool, which in Aramaic is called Bethesda and which is surrounded by five covered colonnades. Here a great number of disabled people used to lie—the blind, the lame, the paralyzed. One who was there had been an invalid for thirty-eight years. When Jesus saw

him lying there and learned that he had been in this condition for a long time, he asked him, "Do you want to get well?" (John 5:1–6)

If someone has been an invalid for thirty-eight years, they most likely have learned to cope, and they probably have taken on the identity of an invalid. If they are healed, their identity is going to change. Some people are afraid to be healed because they know how to cope with their affliction but they do not know how to cope with new challenges that will come if they are healed. Such was the man at the Pool of Bethesda. Jesus knew this, and so He asked the man, "Do you want to get well?" The invalid replied, "I have no one to help me into the pool when the water is stirred. While I am trying to get in, someone else goes down ahead of me" (v. 7).

The man is explaining and complaining at the same time, but he is missing what is really going on. Here is Jesus, the Lord of the angels, the King and Captain of the heavenly hosts, standing before him asking if he wants to get well. And all this man can do is complain about how he is not able to get into the pool when the angel stirs the water. He doesn't know that someone greater than the angel is standing before him. He is focused on the problem rather than the invitation.

I was in Charlotte, North Carolina, and could not find a church that would host our meeting, so we met in a flea market. From ten at night until the last person came in around five in the morning, we ministered. The people who came drove hours to get there. We were getting ready to leave, unaware that a woman with an inoperable brain tumor was about to arrive, when she stepped through the door. Her sister had called and told her that everybody who was prayed for that night had been healed. Not everyone we prayed for was healed that night, but everyone we prayed for after midnight was being healed. This very ill woman got out of bed and came. She took two steps into the flea market, we just barely touched her, and instantly down she went on the floor, out under the power of the Spirit. She could have told her sister, "Just have them pray for me." But she got out of bed and drove for over an hour as an act of faith. She heard her Lord and Savior's invitation, and she acted on it in faith. This wonderful story gives witness to the glory of God. Sadly, not everyone is able to focus on the invitation rather than the problem.

Two months later I returned to Charlotte and held another meeting. The woman who had arrived at 5:00 a.m., who was healed of the brain tumor, came to this second meeting. She told me that all the symptoms associated with the brain tumor had ended that morning when she received prayer. God had healed her.

John Wimber told the story of the time he was at Fuller Seminary conducting a meeting and everyone who received prayer was getting healed. As he was praying for people, he came upon a woman, a missionary in training, who was blind. John told her that everyone who was being prayed for was getting healed. And then he asked, "What do you want us to pray for you?" She replied, "I want you to pray that I will be a good missionary with my blindness." Twice more John told her that everyone who received prayer was being healed and then asked, "What do you want us to pray for you?" And twice more she replied, "I want you to pray that I will be the best missionary I can be with my blindness." John prayed for her, but in accordance with her wishes there was no prayer for her healing from blindness that day, and sadly she continued in her blindness. I believe that God is going to use her, but she could have been healed. God would have used her on the mission field, and she would have had her sight and a wonderful testimony too. She missed the invitation.

"PICK UP YOUR MAT"

Let's return to the Pool of Bethesda. The crippled man and Jesus were beside the pool. The man missed the invitation and focused on the problem as he complained to Jesus about why he had not been healed. "Then Jesus said to him, 'Get up! Pick up your mat and walk.' At once the man was cured; he picked up his mat and walked" (John 5:8–9). Jesus was implying something here. The first thing He told the man to do was to get up. Then He told him to pick up his mat, and then Jesus told him to walk. And the man got up and he walked.

I wonder just how his healing unfolded. Did he all of a sudden begin to feel power? Was he healed after he felt power and that gave him the courage to get up and walk? The scripture does not tell us, but there are implications. The scripture does tell us that Jesus said, "Get up, pick up your mat, and walk." Of course, I cannot prove it, but I think that the man probably didn't feel anything at that point, because that is what I see happen most of the time when I witness healings. That is how I see God work most often. I think he felt no strength in his legs—that nothing happened until he obeyed the first command to get up and walk. I think it was after that first command, when he attempted to get up, that he began to experience his healing.

He was most likely weak at that point. He might have been

questioning all this because he was paralyzed, but when he attempted to get up, he was able to move, to pick up his mat, and walk. I am reading my own interpretation into Scripture, but let's look at the scripture again. Jesus says three things: get up, pick up your mat, and walk. And then the scripture says, "At once the man was cured; he picked up his mat and walked." I believe the healing came when he obeyed and attempted to get up. I believe that faith acted upon in obedience brings the miraculous. But if this wasn't the case with the man and his mat, if the healing came before he obeyed, it is the only one of the miracle signs of Jesus where an act of obedience was not required. The other six instances of the miraculous in John did follow acts of obedience.

RISK

Remember, faith is spelled R-I-S-K. If you play it safe, you may avoid embarrassment, but you won't walk on water. Think about the time Jesus bid Peter to come to Him by walking on the water. When Jesus said, "Come," Peter heard the invitation and acted on it in faith. Now what do you think happened when Peter stuck his foot over the side of the boat and into the water? I don't imagine that the water felt like it was a solid surface. I think that when Peter put his foot over the side of the boat, it just went into the water. I believe that the miracle did not happen until Peter put both feet into the water and began to walk. We will not see the miracle when we still have one foot in the boat, because we are not exercising our faith until we are 100 percent committed to the thing that Jesus tells us to do—when we know there is no turning back.

It wasn't until Peter let go of his faith and began thinking about the reality of his situation that he almost drowned (Matt. 14:30). I read a sermon on this once. The point of the sermon was that if we take risks based on faith, risks that are outside of the norm of the church, we are bound to fail because we do not have the church behind us. We are supposed to stay inside the church, stained glass windows and all, so to speak. I don't agree with this. I think it is the other way around. It is when we are willing to take risks—based on faith and in obedience to God's instructions—that His glory is released in the miraculous. Other than Jesus, Peter is the only person in the Bible to have walked on water. Now that is miraculous! And I believe he thought about that until the day he died.

Peter and the other disciples were imperfect, and we know that because the scriptures portray them that way—especially in John's gospel, which gives details not found in the other gospels. They argued about things like who would sit on the right and the left of Jesus when He came into His kingdom (Mark 10:35–45), and there was the time John and Peter raced each other to the tomb (John 20:4). And we know that it was John who got to lay his head on Jesus' breast at the Lord's Supper (John 13:25). We can see the humanity of these men, and it helps us to grasp the significance of Peter's faith when he walked on the water. These were not super "holy" men. They were ordinary people just like you and me. I appreciate that the Word does not whitewash who these men were.

I have come to know the meaning of risk as I have ministered around the world. I minister in Brazil often, and I can tell you it is hot there. Northern Brazil is very close to the equator, and many of the churches do not have air conditioning. I remember one Sunday morning in particular. I was ministering to a group of about a thousand people, and the sanctuary was hot. It seemed like it got hotter as the worship service continued. At one point I thought, *I have got to end this because we are going to sweat to death!* I knew from experience in this city that at noon the heat would become even more unbearable.

We hadn't had a chance to pray for the sick or give words of knowledge, so I asked the Lord what He wanted me to do, and I was surprised by His response. I felt like the Lord said we were to have everyone stand up and say in unison, "The Lord is good, and His mercy endures forever." We were to repeat that phrase twenty times, then give a mighty shout, and at that point the Lord was going to heal the people. Talk about stepping out of my comfort zone! After years of ministering in Brazil, it has become a place where I feel comfortable taking risks that I would find harder to take at home, so I followed the Lord's leading. We did exactly what He instructed us to do, and God came. Hundreds were healed in a few minutes.

THE GREAT MERCY OF GOD

Let's return to the story of the man who had been paralyzed thirty-eight years. I want to share two insights from this miracle. The first is found in John 5:13. Let us look at it in its context beginning with verse 9.

> At once the man was cured; he picked up his mat and walked. The day on which this took place was a Sabbath, and so the Jewish leaders said to the man who had been healed, "It is the Sabbath; the law forbids you to carry your mat." But he replied, "The man who made me well said to me, 'Pick up your mat and walk.'" So they asked him, "Who is this fellow who told you to

pick it up and walk?" The man who was healed *had no idea who
it was*, for Jesus had slipped away into the crowd that was there.
(vv. 9–13, emphasis mine)

As I've mentioned, this is the only one of the seven miraculous
stories in John that does not make clear there was an act of obedience before the miracle, though I have suggested it is implied. Be
that as it may, there is no indication that this healing resulted in the
man coming to faith in Jesus as a result of his healing. This is the
only miracle of the seven that does not result in a person or people
coming to faith in Jesus. Instead, the remainder of this chapter is
a strong condemnation from Jesus against the unbelief of the Jews
who were aware of the healing of the paralyzed man.

But there is another insight to gain from this story. It has to do
with the content of the man's faith. You will notice that there is no
indication he believed in Jesus. Verses 12 and 13 tell us, "So they
[the Jews] asked him, "Who is this fellow who told you to pick it
up and walk?" The man who was healed *had no idea who it was*, for
Jesus had slipped away into the crowd that was there" (emphasis
mine). There is no indication of this man having a faith for healing
by knowing who Jesus was, because he admitted he had no idea
who it was who had healed him, "for Jesus had slipped away into
the crowd." This healing was a sovereign act on the part of Jesus.
The timing was His, and it happened to be the Sabbath.

Verses 14 and 15 tell us the man later learned it was Jesus who
had healed him, and it is interesting that this was not by accident.
"Later Jesus found him at the temple and said to him, 'See, you are
well again. Stop sinning or something worse may happen to you.'
The man went away and told the Jewish leaders that it was Jesus
who had made him well."

Like the story in John 9 of the man born blind who was healed by Jesus, the blind man also did not know who Jesus was when Jesus told him to go and wash. Yet, he obeyed and was healed. And he, too, was found by Jesus later and came to faith in Him. The formerly paralyzed man seems not to have come to faith in Jesus like the blind man did.

This still happens today. Not everyone who experiences a healing from Jesus comes to saving faith in Him, though many do. Many today do not believe in spite of the testimonies of healing. They are like the Jewish leaders,[2] who knew about the healing of the paralyzed man and knew that Jesus was the One who healed him, yet they did not believe in Jesus. Instead they became hostile to Jesus and believed He was a blasphemer of God instead of the Son of God. Many today who are aware of healings done in Jesus' name reject the healings, refusing to believe they are real or that they come from God. Yet God, in His great love for us and His great mercy, will reach out His mighty hand to heal in spite of our response to Him.

Jesus even said to the man, "See, you are well again. Stop sinning or something worse may happen to you." Yet there seems to have been no interest on this man's part to know more about the One who just healed him. He was so unlike the Samaritan woman at the well, who came to faith in Jesus after He gave her a word of knowledge about her past and present life in regard to her husbands (John 4). The story of the man and his mat leads into Jesus' discourse with the Jewish leaders in which He strongly rebuked their unbelief in the face of the miraculous and talked about the judgment of God on those who refused to believe.

We have studied the first three signs or miraculous events in John.

- The water turned into wine was a miracle of nature brought about by the servants' obedience to Jesus' instructions.
- The royal official's son was healed through the request (prayer) of his father by a spoken declaration of Jesus that included an act of obedience, expressing faith on the part of the father.
- A man who had been paralyzed for thirty-eight years was healed by Jesus, possibly when he tried to get up as an act of faith.

Now let us turn to the other four miracles found in the gospel of John.

SIX

THE RELATIONSHIP OF OBEDIENCE
TO HEALING AND MIRACLES

THE FOURTH MIRACLE I WANT TO EXAMINE IS found in John 6. This is the story of Jesus feeding the five thousand. Jesus and His disciples had just crossed to the far shore of the Sea of Galilee and retreated to a mountainside in an effort to draw away from the huge crowds that were following them as a result of the miraculous signs He had performed on the sick. But the crowds followed them even to the mountainside. John tells us something more about this crowd in verse 2: "And a great crowd of people followed him *because they saw the signs he had performed by healing the sick*" (emphasis mine). Miraculous signs are God's calling card; they create interest and are often used to open people's hearts and minds to the gospel. But, as we saw in the last miraculous story, not all who witness a healing or miracle come to faith. The grace needed to work miracles needs to be followed by the truth of the gospel. Very often miracles are instrumental in bringing people from no interest in Jesus and the gospel to initial interest, then to faith in Jesus and the gospel unto salvation.

Jesus and the disciples began to discuss how they might feed this large crowd. At one point Andrew told Jesus there was a boy with five small barley loaves and two small fish.

> Jesus said, "Have the people sit down." There was plenty of grass in that place, and they sat down (about five thousand men were there). Jesus then took the loaves, gave thanks, and distributed to those who were seated as much as they wanted. He did the same with the fish. When they had all had enough to eat, he said to his disciples, "Gather the pieces that are left over. Let nothing be wasted." So they gathered them and filled twelve baskets with the pieces of the five barley loaves left over by those who had eaten. After the people saw the sign Jesus performed, they began to say, "Surely this is the Prophet who is to come into the world." (John 6:10–14)

This is a mighty miracle. Having often thought about how it happened, I have come up with two possible scenarios that led to it. In the first, Jesus gave each disciple a little bit of bread and a little bit of fish, and when He blessed the food it multiplied, even before the disciples began handing it out. If it had happened that way, it would not have taken any faith on the part of the disciples, and Jesus likes to see us exercise our faith. What I think probably happened was a second scenario, in which Jesus gave each disciple a little bit of bread and a little bit of fish, and it did not begin to multiply until they began handing it out. That's the way I think it happened because the latter took faith.

God has actually confirmed what I believe to be true through the ministry of Rolland and Heidi Baker in Mozambique. At their base in Pemba, the Bakers feed hundreds of orphans every day. Many days they have no idea where the food will come from, yet they continue to trust in the Lord and He continues to provide. There are documented instances when food has multiplied as volunteers were handing it out. Pastor John Arnott's daughter experienced this miracle herself in 2007. Her testimony of multiplication of food can be found in the book titled *Supernatural Missions*.[1]

The Synoptic Gospels tell us that Jesus involved the disciples in the miracle by having them actually distribute the food to the five thousand men. It is not clear whether the miracle happened in their hands as they were distributing or after they obeyed Jesus' instructions to have the people sit down. Perhaps the act of obedience was not on the part of the disciples. Perhaps it happened when the people obeyed the instruction to sit down. Or it could have been both the obedience of the disciples and the people. Regardless, the miraculous multiplication of food followed. The result was that all the people were fed and the disciples collected twelve baskets of leftovers. Again, John is careful to tell us, "After the people saw the miraculous sign that Jesus did, they began to say, 'Surely this is the Prophet who is to come into the world'" (v. 14).

Sadly, there are those who cannot accept the supernatural and go to great lengths to explain it away, often with surprisingly silly explanations. Scottish theologian William Barclay was one of them. While I appreciate Barclay's insights into cultural context, he was a liberal who did not believe that God did supernatural things. Barclay's explanation for how Jesus fed the five thousand is particularly silly. He said that the disciples purchased a large amount of food, found a cool cave, and stored the food in the cave. His explanation for Jesus walking on water was that the water was very shallow and Jesus was standing on solid ground just beneath the water.

Other liberal theologians have proposed that the Red Sea was really the "Reed" Sea, a marshy area about six inches deep, and that strong winds came and blew the water away, hence the "parting of the sea" as told in Exodus 13. I remember hearing this in my Old Testament class in college, raising my hand, and saying, "Still miraculous, still miraculous!" because I contend for the miraculous. How could the Egyptian army have drowned in six inches of water? When you cannot accept the supernatural, you will do crazy things to try to explain it away. We are taught in courses on how to interpret the Bible that we should avoid eisegesis and to do exegesis, which is reading from the text instead of reading into it something it is not saying.

"DO *EXACTLY* WHAT HE SAYS"

I want to look now at John 9:1–2 and 6–11. There is an important principle here that we want to be careful not to miss.

> As he went along, he saw a man blind from birth. His disciples asked him, "Rabbi, who sinned, this man or his parents, that he was born blind?" (vv. 1–2)

After responding to the disciples' question about the cause of the man's blindness and indicating his disagreement with the view it was due to his or his parents' sin,

[Jesus] spit on the ground, made some mud with the saliva, and put it on the man's eyes. "Go," he told him, "wash in the Pool of Siloam" (this word means "Sent"). So the man went and washed, and came home seeing. His neighbors and those who had formerly seen him begging asked, "Isn't this the same man who used to sit and beg?" Some claimed that he was.

Others said, "No, he only looks like him."

But he himself insisted, "I am the man."

"How then were your eyes opened?" they asked.

He replied, "The man they call Jesus made some mud and put it on my eyes. He told me to go to Siloam and wash. So I went and washed, and *then I could see*." (vv. 6–11, emphasis mine)

Think about these passages for a minute. They are a bit strange when you consider them in the natural. Here is a blind man. Jesus just put mud on his eyes and told him to go somewhere specific and wash away the mud. It is not very easy for a blind person to go anywhere. I imagine he was a strange sight with mud in his eyes, trying to make his way to the Pool of Siloam. But this man had the faith to do exactly what Jesus told him to do, and he was healed.

Fast-forward to the late 1900s. A Vineyard team from the Dakotas was ministering in Mexico in a mud hut. They were teaching on the five-step prayer model. (1. Interview/ Diagnosis; 2. Prayer selection; 3. Speak to the condition; 4. Reinterview; 5. Post-prayer recommendation.) One of the indigenous village attendees, there for the training, was legally blind. With the training manual close to his eyes, he was straining to see. He was very poor and had no glasses. One of the Vineyard team members, a teenager, felt at one point that the Lord was saying to put mud on the boy's eyes. At first he questioned if he was really hearing from the Lord or just remembering the scripture. However, he pressed in and felt like the Lord was telling him to do it. So he took some dirt and made mud and put it on the boy's eyes. When his supervisor, a missionary friend of mine, saw what he had done, he was very concerned. He and the others in leadership didn't think it was God. But the teenager, having an impression that he was to wash the boy's eyes, did so and the boy's blindness was instantly healed. At that point, my friend, the missionary, fell on the dirt floor of the hut, weeping with the realization that God had, in fact, spoken to this teenage boy. Obedience—doing exactly what God told him to do—brought the miraculous.

I can recall vividly one of my own moments of exact obedience. Many years ago, when my wife, DeAnne, and I were pioneering a church, we did something we shouldn't have done. We left our nine-year-old son at home alone. We were too poor to afford a babysitter, didn't have any family nearby, and didn't know anyone well enough to ask them to watch our son. None of those are good excuses, but that is what we did. He was actually babysitting his four-year-old sister too! I still feel guilty about this. Nevertheless, at the time I reasoned that we were only a few miles away, and we had given our son a beeper, as this was before cell phones. I told him to beep me if anything went wrong, and we would be home in a matter of minutes.

We were in the middle of a small group meeting in a home and my son, Josh, beeped me. I could hear him gasping on the phone, saying he couldn't breathe. He was having an asthma attack. DeAnne and I hastily explained to the folks at the house meeting what was going on, then we jumped into the car and raced home. When we got to the house, we got a call from a woman at the house meeting named Brenda. Brenda was new to the church and just recently saved. She was not familiar with how the Spirit worked or words of knowledge. As DeAnne was on the phone talking to Brenda, I was praying for Josh. He was very sick and having trouble breathing. My mind was racing, remembering the time his lips and fingertips turned blue and we almost lost him to an asthma attack.

This dear woman was on the phone telling DeAnne that when we left they began praying for us, and she got a mental-impression-type vision that she thought might be from the Lord. In the vision God showed her what we were supposed to do. We were to take two pieces of bread, toast them, and then put them on Josh's chest and cover them with a towel. DeAnne relayed all this to me and asked what I thought. I told her I thought it had to be God because it didn't make any sense. When you think about what we find in the Scripture—talking to a rock to get water, hitting a rock to get water from it, throwing a tree into a lake to purify its water, pointing your stick out to cause the Red Sea to split, putting mud on a man's eyes—then putting two pieces of toast on our son's chest in the middle of an asthma attack doesn't seem quite so crazy. None of it makes sense in the natural, but our God is the God of the supernatural.

Then DeAnne asked me something that illustrates an important principle. She asked if we should butter the toast. Many of you may be smiling at this, but her question is very important because it illustrates a principle that we need to understand if we are to press into the miraculous. We are to do *exactly* what Jesus tells us to do. Brenda did not see us buttering toast in the vision. She made no mention to DeAnne of buttering the toast, and so we were not supposed to do it.

Even though we didn't have a clue what was going on, we followed the Lord's instructions to Brenda exactly. We made the toast and put it on Josh's chest. He was wheezing hard at that point. Then we took a big towel and put it on top of the toast. As soon as the towel touched his chest, he reared up and threw up. I caught everything neatly in the big towel, and Josh was fine after that. I remembered then that the doctors had told us that when someone is in the middle of a severe asthma attack, if you can get them to throw up, their system will release the chemicals necessary to dilate their bronchial tubes. It worked! As crazy as it sounded in the natural, when we followed God's instructions exactly, the miraculous happened.

BELIEVE AND OBEY AND SEE THE GLORY OF GOD

Let's look now at miracle number six in our study, the story of Jesus raising Lazarus from the dead. Lazarus and his sisters, Martha and Mary, were close friends of Jesus. When Lazarus became ill, the sisters sent word to Jesus to come quickly. But Jesus did not go quickly. He purposely waited until Lazarus had died. When he finally arrived, Lazarus had been in the tomb for four days.

> Jesus, once more deeply moved, came to the tomb. It was a cave with a stone laid across the entrance. "Take away the stone," he said. "But, Lord," said Martha, the sister of the dead man, "by this time there is a bad odor, for he has been there four days." Then Jesus said, "Did I not tell you that if you believe, you will see the glory of God?" So they took away the stone. (John 11:38–41)

When I read this passage I am reminded afresh that it is one thing to say we believe but another thing altogether to obey. You have to wonder, what if they had not moved the stone? Perhaps Lazarus would not have been raised from the dead. We need to understand this. Taking away the stone was the revelation that demonstrated their belief even though it went against what they knew in the natural. The stone was removed as Jesus had instructed, and Lazarus was raised from the dead to the glory of God. Obedience in faith brought the glory.

In 1995 I raised a large sum of money to take with me to Russia for a conference. With this money I was able to pay the hotel expenses for a thousand pastors and church planters who had come to the conference. On my team was a Vineyard pastor. He had been praying for an older Russian woman who was basically blind. Even if she held a Bible two inches from her face, she could just barely read it. In the course of praying for this woman, the pastor had an impression to spit in her eyes and God would heal her.

This Vineyard pastor came to me and told me this and then asked me what I thought he should do. He was submitting to me as the leader of the team. My response was to have him ask her if she was comfortable with him spitting in her eyes, and if so, then do it. When he asked her she said, "Yes. Spit!" So he spit in his hands and rubbed it in her eyes, and her eyes opened immediately. By asking her permission, we were allowing her to make the decision, and then we were able to come into agreement with her. There were two acts of obedience: the pastor's and the woman's willingness to say, "Yes. Spit!"

We have to learn to recognize His voice, and sometimes we do that by trial and error. That is why it is important to have a culture of honor in the church if we want to have a culture of the supernatural. We need to learn to honor and encourage one another when we step out in faith, even when we miss the mark. We need to learn to extend grace in the midst of the learning process.

OBEDIENCE WHEN IT MAKES NO SENSE

Now we have come to the last miracle we are going to examine, the story of the miraculous catch of fish. Jesus had died, risen from the dead, and appeared to His disciples in the Upper Room and again later to Thomas. He is about to appear to them yet again, and He is going to reveal Himself through the miraculous. Several of the disciples had been together, fishing throughout the night on the Sea of Tiberius, but they had caught nothing. Early in the morning, as they were returning to shore, Jesus appeared to them, standing on the shore, but they did not realize that it was He.

> He called out to them, "Friends, haven't you any fish?" "No," they answered. He said, "Throw your net on the right side of the boat and you will find some." When they did, they were unable to haul the net in because of the large number of fish. Then the disciple whom Jesus loved said to Peter, "It is the Lord!" (John 21:5–7)

Could it be that they obeyed this stranger on the shore because they remembered the first day that Jesus had called them to be His disciples? They recalled how He had said to them, "Put out into deep water, and let down the nets for a catch" (Luke 5:4). Simon's reply had been, "'Master, we've worked hard all night and haven't caught anything. But because you say so, I will let down the nets.'

When they had done so, they caught such a large number of fish that their nets began to break" (Luke 5:5–6).

The day Jesus stood on the shore calling out to them, they didn't know it was He, but they obeyed. In the natural it couldn't have made much sense. These skilled fishermen had fished all night and caught nothing, yet when they acted on faith, remembering their first encounter with Him, hoping that it was indeed Jesus standing on the shore, a miracle happened.

I believe that is how Jesus calls us to minister today—with faith that He will show up even when our situation doesn't make sense in the natural, even when we think we are hearing from the Lord but we are not sure. I have seen it time and again in my own ministry. When I am willing to risk failure and step out in faith, Jesus shows up with a miracle, confirming my faith.

In 2003 I was in Brazil with a team, preaching to several thousand pastors and leaders. As I was preaching the Lord gave me an impression that I was to take oil and pour it out on the concrete floor and then tell the people that God said, "There is a river of healing right here, like the Pool of Bethesda, and when you come up and stand in this river, I am going to heal you." I strongly believed it was a word from God, and so I set about to consecrate the word by pouring oil on the floor and then inviting the people to come up and be healed. Hundreds responded, coming into the area at the front of the church where the oil had been poured out.

An elderly man came up with severe neuropathy. He could not lift his feet from the floor. All he could do was shuffle with the assistance of a walker. He was also bent over, not because of a bad back, but because of the oppression that was on him. He made his way to the front and got into the "pool," and God started healing him. After a few steps he was able to lift up a heel and then the other heel, more steps, then a foot, and then the other foot. After more steps he started walking normally, without shuffling. And then his back began to straighten up, and his head came up. Hope came upon him, and as it did, it began breaking the oppression. He straightened up tall and continued to take steps, and the people saw what was happening. They began to clap for him and to praise God for the miracle that was happening. And then he threw aside his walker and continued to walk, and the people went crazy with praise. The huge crowd in the "pool" divided, creating a path for the man to walk. Because they had seen him come from the back with his walker, bent over, shuffling his feet until he had reached the pool, there arose a mighty shout of praise to God for the miracle He had worked in this man. There were hundreds more miracles for the people who came to the front to step into the imaginary Pool of Bethesda—the area that had been consecrated by the oil in response to the impression from God.

The man with the walker came in faith and he was healed. What if he hadn't made that effort? What if he had just stayed in the back hoping he would be healed? Would he have been healed anyway? I don't know, but I think it was when he stepped out in faith, literally, that his healing came. And, as I have already said, he wasn't the only one healed in the pool that night. Blind eyes and deaf ears were opened, legs grew out, and many other miraculous healings took place. One of my board members was on this trip, and that night he saw a blind woman healed as he prayed for her.

There was one man who was healed of a massive heart problem. We were in a church with a concrete floor, and the platform upon which he stood to give his testimony of healing was about six feet above the floor. This man got up on the platform, and he was so excited that he lost his balance and fell headfirst onto the floor. He cut his head and broke his arm, but even those injuries couldn't take away his excitement. He came back the following night to tell us that his heart was healed. He didn't care about his broken arm or his busted head because God had given him a new heart—a literal new physical heart to replace the one that had been damaged by a heart attack.

I want to share one last story from the life of William Branham, who was a key leader in the healing revival of 1948 that began in 1946 and some say continued until the early 1960s. His life influenced many men to pursue God for a powerful anointing for healing, including T. L. Osborn, Oral Roberts, Jack Coe, and others. In the course of his years of ministering, he had two vivid visions that contained very explicit instructions to be followed exactly in order to bring about healing. He did everything exactly as he saw it in the visions, and the miraculous followed. He never forgot those experiences. At one point he was invited to St. Louis by a local pastor. In the pastor's church was a child who was bedridden. In a vision God showed Branham exactly what needed to happen for the child to be healed. Upon arriving at the pastor's house, Branham found everything to be exactly as he had seen it in the vision. Encouraged, he did what he believed he was supposed to do according the vision, but the child was not healed. Frustrated, he went over the details of the vision in his mind again and realized that everything had not happened according to the vision. One thing was missing. Before he could pray for the child, a woman was to come through the back door with an umbrella. She would shake the rain out of her umbrella and say, "It is windy out there," and then lay the umbrella up against the door. It was at that point that Branham was supposed to go to the child, say the prayer the Lord had given him, and she would be healed.

Knowing what he was supposed to do now, Branham settled down and waited. After a time a woman came through the back door, shook her umbrella, said, "It is windy out there," and then laid the umbrella up against the door. At that point Branham got up, went to the child and prayed, and the child was healed.

There is something about obedience that the Lord wants us to understand, and it is this—*do exactly as He says!* Because when we do, He will meet us at our point of need and reveal His glory. If we, the church, learn how to become intimate with Jesus, the King of glory, stepping out in faith, believing that God is who He says He is, and acting in obedience to His word, we will surely see a release of the miraculous.

> "And I will do whatever you ask in my name, so that the Father may be glorified in the Son. You may ask me for anything in my name, and I will do it." (John 14:13–14)

This teaching on acts of obedience is what I call a diamond teaching. It has one point—*do whatever He says*—and many facets. I pray you are encouraged as you step out in faith, taking risks and in faith believing that God is who He says He is. In the next chapter we will consider some modern illustrations of such acts of obedience from the lives of other ministers who have healing ministries and from former interns of mine who now have their own itinerate ministries, are pastoring, or who serve as missionaries. We will also examine the relationship between obedience and glory, turning to the book of Colossians and Paul's teaching on the mystery that has been kept hidden but is now disclosed: that Christ indwells every believer, Jew and Gentile alike, for every believer is made perfect in Christ.

SEVEN

CHRIST IN YOU, THE HOPE OF GLORY

I DID A WORD STUDY ON *GLORY* AS IT IS FOUND IN both the Old and New Testaments (NIV). I was intrigued by the results. By far the largest category in this study is healings and miracles. I found glory associated with healings sixteen times and with miracles fourteen times, for a total of thirty times. There are more references to glory associated with healings and miracles than with anything else in the Bible. The most frequent single reference to glory in the Bible is associated with a cloud—the cloud of glory or the glory cloud. I found the cloud of glory twenty-three times in the Scriptures. Compared to the category of healings and miracles, it is the second most frequently mentioned category in the Bible.

I also found glory associated with the future state of the presence of God twelve times, with fire eleven times (and this is important especially when we understand that He makes His angels "winds" and His servants "flames of fire"), as a synonym for *power* nine times (primarily by the apostle Paul), and as light or radiance eight times. There are eight references to glory associated with suffering (in the context of persecution, not sickness and disease) and another eight references to glory associated with the worship of all nations (all nations shall see His glory).

I found glory associated with angels seven times, with judgment five times, and with God's house three times. And that's not all.

Scripture references glory as ministry to the poor, revelation of God's name, consecration, setting the borders of Israel, illuminating a rainbow, and being too deep to comprehend. Glory is a major theme of the Bible. As the people of God, we are called to give Him glory. In the context of the ministry of healing, we need look no further than Jesus' ministry for our example of how to do this. Through healings and miracles and signs and wonders, Jesus continually gave glory to His Father during His ministry on this earth, and He continues to do this as we minister in His name with miracles, signs, and wonders today. The early church was built in large part through the miraculous signs, wonders, healings, and miracles that demonstrated the power of God as greater than any other spiritual power.[1]

We are called to do no less today, and yet sadly much of the church has labored under the wrong teaching that healings and miracles, signs and wonders are not for modern times. Through incorrect doctrine we have almost succeeded in rendering the church a powerless institution. But it is not too late to recover the emphasis upon our privilege—the privilege of who we are in Jesus Christ and who Jesus Christ is in us. It is not too late for us to have faith—faith that the Spirit in us is the hope of glory![2] To fully engage this privilege we have been given, we must understand and embrace the reality that we are a priesthood of believers. We are all priests under God. We're a royal priesthood, a holy nation (1 Peter 2:5, 9). Christ in each of us is the hope of glory (Col. 1:27). And we must make no mistake—the devil fights hard against the concept of the priesthood of believers. Why? Because when we understand this concept, when we understand our privilege, we are able to co-labor with Christ, with all His energy that works so mightily within us,[3] to restore His kingdom here on earth.

It is my hope and prayer that as we examine glory together, the Holy Spirit will create in you a greater hunger and thirst to press into the fullness of the knowledge of Christ in you, the hope of glory, so that you may experience a greater empowering for His kingdom work.

LET SCRIPTURE SPEAK FOR ITSELF

I want to give you an interpretation of Colossians 1:25–29 that is not the traditional interpretation. While I believe the traditional interpretation is possible, I think it is insufficient to explain all that happened at the cross and the meaning of mystery in this passage. To capture everything that happened at the cross, we need a bigger view; and to get this bigger view we must first remove the reformational lenses of Luther and Calvin and let the text speak for itself so that it is not being interpreted through a lens that's a reaction to Catholicism. Paul wrote to the Colossians:

I have become its servant by the commission God gave me to present to you the word of God in its fullness—the mystery that has been kept hidden for ages and generations, but is now disclosed to the Lord's people. To them God has chosen to make known among the Gentiles the glorious riches of this mystery, *which is Christ in you, the hope of glory.* He is the one we proclaim, admonishing and teaching everyone with all wisdom, so that we may present everyone fully mature in Christ. *To this end I strenuously contend with all the energy Christ so powerfully works in me.* (Col. 1:25–29, emphasis mine)

The Upper Room Discourse in John has definite parallels to the Colossians 1:25–29 passage, with John and Paul emphasizing the ability of the followers of Jesus to have intimacy with Him and to recognize His communications to them. The Holy Spirit in us enables us to receive these communications and is the source of the power that flows out of us to bring glory to God by healing or delivering people of sickness, disease, accidents, or demons. Jesus died, rose, and ascended in order to inaugurate the new covenant in the power of the Spirit. What a privilege we are given to partner with our risen Lord and Savior, to share the lifesaving message of the gospel with signs and wonders following so that all may hear and come safely into the arms of the Good Shepherd.

The Roman Catholic Church has historically had a much more biblical view of healing than many Protestant denominations, believing that healings and miracles still occur today, while holding to the "proof of doctrinal orthodoxy" view that says the primary purpose of miracles is the evidence of true doctrine. While the Catholic Church was saying, "miracles prove our doctrine," Protestants, in their quest for authority, threw out present-day miracles, saying, "We don't need any miracles, because the real miracles that are authenticating doctrine are in the Bible, and once the Bible was canonized there was no further need for miracles." To this Protestant way of thinking, a continuation of miracles would allow new doctrine to be added to Scripture. Out of this historical context comes the negative view of healing that we find in much of the church today. I don't agree with this position. I don't believe that the primary purpose of miracles is to authenticate doctrine.

If you look at Martin Luther's writings, you will see that he favored the Gospel of John more than Matthew, Mark, or Luke because the book of John only has seven miracles in it. Matthew, Mark, and Luke are full of miracles. Likewise, he gravitated to the Epistles over the Gospels because the Epistles have fewer miracles. Among the Reformers, Calvin's theology was most committed to cessationism. Cessationism is the view that the offices of apostles, prophets, and evangelists—as well as the gifts of tongues, interpretation of tongues, gifts of healings, working of miracles, and prophecy—have ceased. But in fairness to both Luther and Calvin, there was a degree of comfortableness with the miraculous in their ministries. This can be seen in the seemingly miraculous gift of faith Luther experienced when praying for healing of two other significant Lutheran Reformers, Philip Melanchthon and Friederick Myconius. It could also be seen in Calvin's belief that in regions of the world where there was no church, the apostles', prophets', and evangelists' offices could occur again to establish the church, but once it was established the offices would again disappear.[4]

On October 30, 1517, Martin Luther nailed his Ninety-five Theses to the door of the Wittenberg Church in Germany and the Reformation "officially" began. Neither Luther nor Calvin ever challenged the Aquinas-Aristotelian[5] synthesis in their writing. Despite his philosophical bias, in 1540 Luther successfully prayed for his fellow reformer and systematizer of Lutheran doctrine, Philip Melanchthon, to be healed as he lay near death. Instead of a "thy will be done" approach, Luther found a "my will be done" declaration. How interesting. It is sad that so few Lutherans are aware of this side of Luther's ministry. The following occurred July 2, 1540.

Melanchthon was on his way to the scene of these deliberations when, brooding over this unhappy affair, his fears and scruples brought on a sickness just as he had reached Weimar, which laid him nigh to death's door. Intelligence of his state was conveyed to Wittenberg, and Luther, in the Elector's carriage, hastened to Weimar. He found Philip, on his arrival, apparently all but dead; understanding, speech, and hearing had left him, his countenance was hollow and sunk, his eyes closed, and he seemed in a death-like sleep. Luther expressed his astonishment to the companions of his journey, "How shamefully has the devil handled this creature!" and then, according to his custom, turning to the window, he prayed with all his might. *He reminded God of his promises from the Holy Scriptures, and implored him now to fulfill them, or he could never trust in them again.*[6] Rising from prayer he took Melanchthon's hand and called to him in a cheerful tone, "Take heart, Philip: you shall not die. God has reason enough to kill you, but 'He willeth not the death of the sinner, but rather that he should repent and be saved.' He desires life, not death. The greatest sinners that ever lived on earth—Adam and Eve— were accepted of God in his grace; far less will he give you up, Philip, and let you perish in your sins and faintheartedness. Give no room to despondancy: be not your own murderer; but throw yourself on your Lord, who killeth and maketh alive." At these words Melanchthon evinced a sudden restoration, as though from death to life; he drew his breath with energy; and after a while turning his face to Luther, implored him "not to stay him; he was on a good journey; and nothing better could befall him." Luther replied, "Not so, Philip, you must serve our Lord God yet longer." And when Melanchthon had gradually become more cheerful, Luther, with his own hands, brought him something to eat, and overruled his repugnance with the threat, "Hark, Philip, you shall eat, or I excommunicate you."[7]

Lutheran reformer and intimate friend of Martin Luther, Friedrich Myconius (1490–1546) was sick and about to die, rapidly sinking in consumption. Myconius sent word to Luther that he "was sick, not for death, but for life." Luther commenced to pray fervently that Myconius "might not pass through the veil to rest, whilst he was left out-of-doors amid the devils," and wrote to his friend that he felt certain his prayers would be heard, and by God's mercy his days would be lengthened, so that he would survive Luther. Myconius was raised up again from the brink of the grave, and eventually outlived Luther by seven weeks.[8]

Luther's prayer ended with, "Farewell dear Friedrich. The Lord grant that I may not hear of your departure while I am still living. May he cause you to survive me. This I pray. This I wish. *My will be done.* Amen. For it is not for my own pleasure but for the glory of God's name that I wish it."[9]

Sometime later Luther remarked about this time of prayer for Friedrich and Philip. After snatching Philip from the arms of death, Luther described his bold prayer: "In this instance our Lord God had to pay me; for I threw the bag of concern before his door and I dinned his ears with all of his promises as to how he desired to favorably hear our prayer—promises which I well knew how to document in Scripture! I put it to him that he had to grant my request if he expected me to continue to trust his promises."[10]

While looking for the quote of Luther's prayer for Myconius, I discovered a very interesting book written in 1832 called *The Suppressed Evidence: Or Proofs of the Miraculous Faith and Experience of the Church of Jesus Christ in All Ages* by the Reverend Thomas

Boys, MA, of Trinity College, Cambridge. It, too, gives evidence that even the Reformers themselves believed in miracles and in the possibility of miracles occurring in their time.[11]

Calvin believed that if you took the gospel into a place where it had never been heard before, you could expect miracles to happen again until the church was established, at which point miracles would cease.[12] This Calvinist view says that once the church is established you didn't *need* miracles anymore.[13] If that were the case, churches today would be bursting at the seams, and the moral fabric of societies would look like a lovely tapestry of the kingdom. If that were the case, the church would be a beautiful reflection of Jesus in the world to the glory of God. Sadly, that is not the case for much of the church. When a powerless gospel is preached, the church finds itself increasingly marginalized and maligned, with hungry hearts turning to ungodly choices in pursuit of truth, beauty, and the power to live an overcoming life. Yet not all of the church reflects such a bleak picture. When the full gospel is taught and demonstrated, the church comes alive in the world with salvations, healings, and deliverance that brings the abundant life God intends for each one of us.

THE TRADITIONAL INTERPRETATION

Let's begin by looking at the traditional interpretation of Colossians 1:25–29. The mainline evangelical understanding of this passage is that the anointing of God, or God's Spirit in me, is my hope of glory in the sense of having a glorified body and experiencing glory in the next life, after the second coming. This interpretation has an eschatological meaning, an end-time meaning. I believe that the glory of God upon us and in us is our down payment, our guarantee that in the end we will have and receive a glorified body in the general resurrection at the end of time. This is good news. I am a child of God, and I believe that His Spirit in me is my hope of having a glorified body, but I don't think this exhausts the meaning of this passage. Actually, I don't believe it is the principal meaning of this passage.

In mainline Protestantism most all the promises of Scripture are not for now. They will happen in the millennial reign of Christ or after the second coming of Jesus, but not now. This view is what I call "underrealized eschatology." This futuristic view is the traditional interpretation of Colossians 1:25–29.

BEYOND THE TRADITIONAL INTERPRETATION

Now we're going to move beyond this traditional understanding, and I'm going to give you another way of looking at the text. I'm not throwing out the traditional interpretation, but adding to it. And I don't stand alone with my interpretation. Other theologians and scholars agree with me, but the great majority of biblical commentaries only present the traditional understanding. We will begin with reviewing Scripture itself.

I have become its [the church, the body of Christ's] servant by the commission God gave me to present to you the word of God in its fullness—the mystery that has been kept hidden for ages and generations, but is now disclosed to the Lord's people. To them God has chosen to make known among the Gentiles the glorious riches of this mystery, which is Christ in you, the hope of glory. (Col. 1:25–27)

In this passage a revelation is given. God has pulled back the curtain and revealed something that was previously unavailable to us. The mystery that was hidden is now disclosed. There are actually two mysteries revealed in this text. One mystery is that God was grafting the Gentiles into the Jewish trunk. This was shocking to the Jews. A Gentile was considered no better than a dog by the Jews, and now God was revealing that His kingdom was available to the Gentiles also, not just the Jews. Many could not accept this.

The second mystery is the revelation that the Holy Spirit was to be poured out on *all* flesh. Jesus, the Christ, the anointed One, the Messiah would be available to both Jew and Gentile. This was also shocking news to the Jews. God sent Jesus that *all* might be saved and filled with His presence and power. In my book *Baptized in the Spirit*,[14] theologian Dr. Jon Ruthven advocates for a move toward a doctrine of the baptism of the Spirit that is emphasized in the Bible, toward the use of the term as Jesus presented it. In this view, the baptism of the Spirit is not simply an optional add-on to salvation but the very goal of the Bible, the central experience of the new covenant, and the ideal expression of a truly Christian disciple.[15] "We should gladly receive all that we have access to through Holy Spirit baptism, laying aside doctrinal hindrances and pressing into the fulness of the mighty power from on high that is ours through Christ Jesus." F. F. Bosworth says, "God is waiting to pour out the Holy Spirit in fulness upon us. He comes as Christ's executive to execute for us all the blessings provided by Calvary."[16]

What do these blessings look like in the world today? The following testimony is from another Global Awakening Theological

Seminary student, Benjamin Stewart. Ben is a pastor's son, raised in one of the largest Vineyard churches in Canada. In 1994, at the tender age of nine, Ben was radically touched by the Holy Spirit during a visit to the Toronto Airport Christian Fellowship church. This encounter set him on a lifelong journey of serving the Lord. In addition to his studies, Ben is currently the director of events for Global Awakening. The following story from Ben gives witness that the blessing provided by Calvary looks like Jesus.

While working for a missions and development organization, I was on assignment in a small village in Uganda filming a documentary to raise awareness for a large community transformation project we were about to undertake. On my second day of filming, I was walking through a village hospital, which was little more than seven concrete rooms with no electricity or power. Crowded into these rooms were hundreds of men, women, and children waiting to see a village doctor who had little medicine. As I made my way through the hospital, the desperation of the people was palpable. Cries of pain and anguish could be heard coming from every direction. Entering the last room on the left, I found an older woman lying on a bed holding a girl covered in sweat, unconscious, with an IV tube disconnected and hanging from her arm. While I had seen a great deal of sickness and pain in my ten or fifteen minutes in the hospital, this particular woman, weeping over this seemingly lifeless girl, filled me with overwhelming compassion, and I knew I needed to stop filming and pray for her.

I called for my translator and asked the woman the girl's name. It was Sarah, and the woman was her grandmother. She explained that she had brought her granddaughter in the day before with a fever, diarrhea, vomiting, and loss of appetite, fearing for her granddaughter's life. The doctors told her that her granddaughter had advanced malaria and she was immediately given the bed she was now in and placed on an IV. Shortly after she arrived, Sarah lost consciousness and failed to regain it. An hour or so before I arrived, the doctors had told her that the medicine was not working and that there was nothing they could do to save her granddaughter, that Sarah would be dead by morning. They were short of medicine and could waste no more trying to save the girl. They would have to remove the IV but would allow the woman to remain there with her granddaughter until she died. As she told me this, I could see that Sarah's breathing was labored and somewhat spastic. Sarah was sweating profusely, her eyes were moving under her eyelids, and she showed no signs of responding to my voice or being conscious of her surroundings. The situation was dire. I told the grandmother that I was a Christian and that God had sent me here to pray for Sarah. I asked if she would allow me to pray. The woman told me that she, too, was a believer and that she attended the local church. She welcomed my prayers.

At this point, I didn't consider how to pray; I simply dove into praying for Sarah. My motivation was the compassion I felt, and that drove an internal battle where I felt the injustice her death would be. Simply put, had she lived in the developed world or had access to better medical care, she would have lived. I felt the Enemy was robbing her life, and something inside of me said, *I'm not going to let that happen.* Considering that now, it sounds like hubris, but at the time it was merely conviction.

I placed a hand on Sarah's head; it was burning up. "Holy Spirit, come now and fill Sarah," I prayed. I waited a few moments. "Come, Holy Spirit, come." I waited a bit longer. I could sense the anointing in the room. I can't be sure if the place became quieter—it was quite chaotic with many sick people filling the room—or if there was a focus that came as the anointing came on Sarah, her grandmother, the translator, and me. Whichever it was, as the anointing came on us, it was as though we were alone.

I continued to pray: "I take authority over this fever in Sarah's body, and I command it to go now in Jesus' name. I speak to her body, and I tell it to regulate its temperature now in Jesus' name. I speak to this infection, and I say go now in Jesus' name. I speak to her immune system, and I say come alive in Jesus' name. I speak to malaria, and I say go now in Jesus' name. I speak to the assignment of death over Sarah, and I say death, you have no hold on Sarah. We plead the blood of Jesus Christ over her. We speak life into her cells. We speak life into her immune system. We speak life into her body. We say arise in Jesus' name."

At this point, there was a sense of breakthrough. It is hard to describe precisely; Sarah didn't open her eyes, but something broke in the spirit. Her grandmother started to thank Jesus in Luganda. I began thanking Jesus as well. I looked at Sarah, and while the undergarments she was wearing were still wet, her forehead began to dry, and her breathing seemed to come more easily. There was a calm in her body that hadn't been there before. Her grandmother had tears in her eyes, as did the translator; something significant had shifted. I felt Sarah's forehead, and it was no longer burning up, and her eyes had stopped moving under her eyelids; they were steady. While her body had been in a state of panic moments before, it now was calm, as though she were sleeping peacefully.

I felt certain Sarah was healed and we had received the breakthrough. I encouraged Sarah's grandmother to ask the doctors to reexamine Sarah. She told me that she would try but they probably wouldn't. I knew that this was likely the case but encouraged her to try regardless. I said to her that Sarah's fever had broken, which she could see, and that she was now resting. She agreed. I said she should continue to hold her and to report back to the pastor if there was any change in Sarah's condition. I then instructed her to watch Sarah closely, and if the fever tried to return, to break it off, break the assignment of death, and speak life into her body. I told her she had as much authority as a believer in Jesus as I did. I blessed her and prayed for peace over her and moved on to pray for others.

The next day after preaching in the church, I was told that Sarah woke up and asked for something to eat. I was reminded of Jesus' healing of Jairus' daughter. A few months later, I returned to the village and was greeted by Sarah and her grandmother with a massive hug. I have been back to Uganda many times, as recently as June 2019, and have seen Sarah grow up to be a brilliant and wonderful young woman. She loves the Lord, and she and her grandmother have never stopped thanking me for my prayer, most recently thanking me with the gift of a beautiful chicken, which was delicious.

I have used this story in sermon illustrations about compassion for years. I believe that the compassion I felt was the same as Jesus felt for this girl; it was not mine but His. I think that this was the Father's way of commanding me to heal

Sarah: by filling me with a sense of gut-wrenching compassion. Interestingly, I had never seen it as a word of knowledge until a conversation with Dr. Randy Clark a few weeks ago.

He asked me the question, "Why that girl? Why in a hospital filled with overwhelmingly sick people did you feel compassion for that one girl?" When I didn't have an answer, he responded that he believed it was a word of knowledge that God had given me in the form of compassion. I now think that this is true. When I replay the scene in my mind, I see that I was confronted by literally hundreds of desperately ill people, many of whom I ended up praying for after, a few of whom were also healed—but it was Sarah that I felt I *had* to stop and pray for. It was a special compassion from God. So while this does not fit into the traditional list of ways words of knowledge typically come for healing, it was indeed a powerful word of knowledge that led to a powerful miracle.

Jesus healed the sick as proof that the kingdom of heaven had come to earth. When I felt a sense of justice rise up in me, I was partnering with Jesus in this, and in His purpose of defeating the works of the devil. While it was an act of compassion and justice for me, to Sarah and her grandmother it was an act of God's love, and it bonded us together in love. This love is expressed each time we see each other; we are united in the love of God, rooted in our shared experience of Sarah's healing.

Christ living in Ben was the source of this miracle. Christ in us was, is, and will always be our hope of glory, our hope of experiencing the power of God to reveal, heal, deliver, and make whole someone who is in need. This is the mystery that was made known to the church: Jew and Gentile alike could experience the living presence of the triune God in us, the One who works so mightily through us with His energy. Ben is not the one who healed Sarah—Jesus in Ben is the One who healed Sarah. It should be pointed out that the unity in the Trinity enabled Paul to interchangeably use titles like Holy Spirit, Spirit of God, Spirit of Jesus. It is also the reason Jesus said that when the *Paracletos* (Holy Spirit) came into a person's life, the Father and the Son have also come.

EIGHT

THE GLORY AND THE CROSS

THE CONCEPT OF GLORY IN THE BIBLE IS ABOUT more than the state of being glorified, as in our "glorified bodies" that we will receive upon the second coming of Christ when He returns and establishes His rule and reign on the earth. If this were the only meaning of glory, then glory would only be in the future. It would not be available to us in the present. And if glory is not available to us in the present, the gospel has no emphasis on healing or deliverance. It becomes like term life insurance—you have to die to get the benefits. Without glory, we have no hope in this world, only in the next. Karl Marx, the founder of communism, dubbed religion the "opiate of the people" in an 1843 book on philosophical criticism, saying Christians preached "pie in the sky," rather than a hope for the present.[1] That's the kind of thinking that can come out of the traditional interpretation of the Colossians 1:25–29 passage we discussed in the last chapter.

When we look at the cross through the lens that most conservative evangelical Protestants Christians use today, the predominant understanding of the death of Jesus is found in the doctrine of substitutionary atonement. "He made Him who knew no sin to be sin for us, that we might become the righteousness of God in Him" (2 Cor. 5:21 NKJV). Jesus is the substitute. He's the Lamb of God who was slain (John 1:29; 1 Cor. 5:7). He bore in His body our sins, our sicknesses, and our diseases (Isa. 53:4–5). As *the* substitutionary atonement, He died so that we wouldn't have to (Rom. 5:8). This is the main understanding of the cross, particularly for Protestants, that Jesus' death allows us to not perish but have eternal life, because it is a substitutionary atonement for our sins.[2] Morris deals with the theory of atonement in *The Cross in the New Testament*, sees value in all of the theories, but believes the aspect of substitution is vital to the teaching of the cross in the New Testament.[3]

I believe in the doctrine of substitutionary atonement. It is wonderful. And because of what Jesus did on the cross, we can approach God in our time of need (Heb. 4:16). But I also believe that this understanding of the cross is insufficient to capture everything the cross represents. If we are to really capture everything that happened at the cross, we need a bigger view. To get to this bigger view we must return to the understanding of the cross for the first one thousand years of the church. I'm talking about a biblical, scriptural understanding of the cross.

The primary concept of what Jesus did on the cross, for the first one thousand years of Christianity, is now known as *Christus Victor*.[4] *Christus Victor* says that because Jesus died on the cross, in our place, God raised Him from the dead and gave Him power over all powers. And because of His resurrection, He defeated the Enemy and He has now ascended to the Father's right hand. And He has poured out the Holy Spirit on us. In Jesus we have victory over disease, demons, and death *in the present*. We don't have to die to get these benefits. The benefits of the cross are available to us right now while we're alive, to heal our bodies and to give us victory over demonic oppression. This was the teaching of the early church. *Christus Victor* is not an "either/or"; it's a "both/and" understanding that includes traditional substitutionary atonement.

But the secondary understanding of the early church (that Jesus died so we can go to heaven) became the predominant understanding today. This switch occurred during the Protestant Reformation, and it arose because of the problem of miracles. Miracles caused a problem of authority. The Roman Catholic Church taught that miracles still occurred, and these miracles authenticated their doctrines. Protestants also held the perspective that miracles authenticate doctrines. Since they believed some Catholic doctrines had departed from the New Testament, they concluded the miracles can't authenticate false doctrines; therefore those miracles the Catholics referred to must be false or counterfeit miracles. The best way to get around this problem of authority was to say that miracles don't happen anymore. And if they don't happen anymore, they can't be the emphasis of the gospel that the classic view of the atonement, *Christus Victor*, referred to for the first thousand years of the church's history.

I think it is time that we, the church, see the bigger view that the early church saw. When we look at the bigger view, this scripture can mean something more. Why do we think all the benefits of the cross have to be in the future and not now also? Some say this is an overrealized eschatology—that we are expecting in the present those things that are reserved for the future, the end times. My response is, "No, I'm not guilty of an overrealized eschatology. You're guilty of an underrealized present reality." The present reality of who God is as Christ in us, in you and me, is the hope of glory—our hope for God to be glorified on the earth as we allow the supernatural of God, deposited in us by the finished work of the cross, to impact the world through ministry and mission. Keeping it simple makes it easier to engage His supernatural in everyday life. The following testimony from Brian Starley, one of my associates and presently a student in my eight-week Christian Healing course at Global Awakening Theological Seminary, illustrates this point.

In our journey of following God's voice, we can easily develop a habit of limiting how and when He speaks to us. The truth is, He is always near, whether at a church service or on the streets. As we make ourselves available, He will speak to us and use us to impact others. I received this word of knowledge as I walked over to my local gym, not in a conference or an overtly spiritual setting. As I was on my way to the gym, I passed in front of a sushi restaurant. While I was walking by, two men exited the building. Just as they were leaving, I was fumbling in my pockets and dropped my membership card onto the ground. I reached down to pick it up, but before I could, one of the men had already retrieved it. He handed the card back to me, and as he did, our hands touched for a split second. As soon as I made physical contact with him, I felt a deep sense of anxiety come over me, with a simultaneous clenching in my chest. Feeling other people's pains and emotions is one of the ways that words of knowledge come to us.

Right after I experienced this feeling of anxiety and chest pain, I knew it was for one of the two men. The reason I knew this is because I do not have either of these symptoms in the natural. I began by thanking him for helping me, followed by introducing myself and asking for his name. I could tell that he thought this was strange. After all, most people will not usually start a conversation over something so small. However, he answered and told me his name was Andrew. From there, I knew what I said next would seem like a very odd question. I warned him about it being unusual and said that I would explain why I was asking afterward. I then asked, "Would you happen to be suffering from a lot of anxiety?" He had a look of both shock and confusion and responded to me, "Isn't everyone anxious right now?"

I could tell by both his response and his body language that he was feeling uncomfortable. I explained to him that I am a Christian. I said, "Sometimes God gives me insight into people's lives, and I often pray for them to receive healing." After I said this, he became much more relaxed and interested. Suddenly I felt the presence of the Holy Spirit come upon me, and I knew that God wanted to speak to Andrew. I have found that as I minister, I often feel a strong bubbling-up sensation before a revelatory word comes. In my estimation, about 90 percent of the time, the words that follow will be accurate.

I said to Andrew, "To answer your question, I know that many are struggling with anxiousness right now. But I believe this is specific to you. I feel like you were suffering long before this COVID-19 pandemic with fear due to your college major. You want to change your degree and have been terrified of your father's disapproval. Not only that, but you are afraid of choosing the wrong path. It has even started to create a lot of pain in your chest from extreme stress. God wants you to know that He sees your desire for being an entrepreneur, and He is going to bless you as you pursue business." When I finished speaking, Andrew's eyes filled with tears. He said that all this was true, and he could not believe what he was hearing. I told him it was because of God's love for him and asked if I could pray. He quickly agreed, only asking if I could do so without touching him.

Because of the revelation that God gave, and Andrew confirming it to be accurate, I believed I had a precise diagnosis, so to speak, that Andrew was suffering from severe fear and anxiety that was causing emotional distress. This anxiety was also causing physical pain in his chest. I felt the Holy Spirit leading me to pray a commanding prayer for the spirit of fear to be broken. Often I will ask more questions, but I did not feel led to inquire any further at the time, so I said to Andrew, "I won't need to touch you. I'll just stand here, pray out loud, and wait." I told him that he would not need to pray with me or to do any set of activities. I remember specifically saying, "You don't need to do anything but relax; you can close your eyes and just focus on what is happening."

I invited the Holy Spirit to come and meet us and then began praying. I prayed, "Lord, thank You for Andrew. Thank You for Your love for him. I bless you, Andrew. In the name of Jesus, I break the power of the spirit of fear. I command you to leave Andrew, and I speak the peace of God over his life." As I prayed with my eyes open, I watched as the signs of God's healing presence were taking place. Andrew was crying heavily, and I noticed trembling in his left hand. The prayer was then interrupted, in the best sense of that word. His friend, who had been waiting in the car, quickly walked over when he noticed what was happening. Although I am not positive what he was thinking, it looked like he was mostly shocked by the situation.

As soon as he reached where we were standing, Andrew's friend's right leg began twitching. This was before any of us spoke to him about what was happening. He had no idea what was going on, and his attention was quickly diverted away from Andrew and onto his leg. While Andrew was still being visibly touched by God, I turned to his friend. His confusion was elevated now that his leg was shaking. I knew something was happening, but I was unsure what.

I felt that the wise choice was just to ask him if anything was wrong with his leg. I believe that this was much better than trying to stop and explain everything to him. I asked, "Is there anything wrong with your leg?" To which he replied, "I injured my ACL playing soccer about a decade ago, and it never healed correctly. Right now, I don't know what is going on with it!" I tried to calm him down, letting him know that I was a Christian who was praying for his friend. His leg continued to move, like an intense muscle spasm in appearance.

We know that there are various signs, such as heat and shaking, which indicate that God is moving. I was about to ask if I could pray for his leg when I felt a sudden urge not to do so. I felt like God interrupted me and said that He was healing it apart from my prayer. I have learned to pay attention to impressions like these and act on them. I learned from Randy the importance of declaring what you believe to be true. We speak to demonstrate that we have faith in the *rhema* word. I asked him to try and do something that he could not do before. As he started to put a great deal of pressure on his leg, he looked up at me with his eyes widened. He said, "You've got to be kidding me!"

I asked him what was happening, and he said that the pain he usually felt was not there whatsoever. I then asked him to keep trying more things out, and he proceeded to run back and forth on the sidewalk. He even did squats and jumped to put more force onto the injury. God had entirely healed his complications from the ACL tear! At this point, both he and Andrew were in tears. Andrew was not only encountering God himself, he had just witnessed his friend get healed too.

What God did through young Brian He did as a result of Christ in him the hope of glory, and the energy Christ so powerfully worked in Brian to reveal information and release power to heal these two young men. I know Brian's story. It is an amazing story of God's grace coming on him to regenerate him. Baptized in the power of the Holy Spirit, Brian has a great desire to learn how to hear the leadings of the Lord—words of knowledge—and continues to pursue a greater understanding of the ways of God. Brian heard the Lord tell him to come to the Global School of Supernatural Ministry for two years. When I saw his character and the anointing on him (Christ in him), I invited him to become my intern for a year and then to become a full-time minister in my ministry's organization—the Apostolic Network of Global Awakening.

Brian's story is typical of almost every one of my associates and the approximately sixty people I have personally mentored as interns. Brian didn't start out with such accuracy. He practiced trying to hear the Lord, and in the beginning there were lots of misses. Through much practice, in time, he was more able to clearly discern the difference between his thoughts and the thoughts initiated by

Christ in him. This is the privilege of every Christian. Christ in you is the basis for you to have hope for similar experiences. Jesus said, "My sheep hear my voice" (John 10:27 KJV).

THE NEW COVENANT FULFILLED

Let's examine the remainder of Colossians 1:28–29, beginning at verse 28.

> He is the one we proclaim, admonishing and teaching everyone with all wisdom, so that we may present everyone fully mature in Christ. To this end I strenuously contend with all the energy Christ so powerfully works in me.

The energy Paul is speaking of here is not to be limited to the energy of God that is going to come and give us glorified bodies at the end of time. Paul is talking about God's energy being available to us right now. Paul labored with God's energy working powerfully within him. We, too, strenuously contend, right now, with all His energy that works so powerfully within us. We co-labor with Christ, not in our own power but with His energy. The anointing of the Holy Spirit (God's energy) in us is the same anointing that was in and with Jesus Christ (John 14:23). It's the same power Jesus operated in. Jesus told us it was to our advantage that He go away, because when He went away He was able to send the Holy Spirit. It is the Holy Spirit, the Spirit of truth that guides us into all truth, speaking not on His own but only what He hears, bringing glory to God (John 16:5–16). In this way Jesus comes back to us and is able to be with all His people, everywhere, at all times.

The anointing of the Spirit of Jesus is in us through the unity of the Trinity. Jesus essentially tells us, "I'm going to be in you, and my Father and I are going to be in you, and the Spirit is going to be in you, and this is the hope of glory." This is the mystery that has been hidden that has now been revealed: that the power of God is no longer just coming upon priests and kings and judges but upon every believer in the new covenant. The new covenant is being fulfilled. The power of the Spirit is coming, and He is on us now. The kingdom of God can be advanced through me and you, and the gates of hell shall not prevail against us (the church).[5] What are the gates of hell? Paul said the god of this world is the devil. And Jesus came to serve him notice of trespassing. His kingdom is being leavened by the leaven of the gospel[6] as the church goes forward.

As a kid I used to think that the church was "here" and the gates of hell were "out there," that the church was in a defensive position. But I was a little country boy, and I was wrong. I don't know where I got it. Maybe it had something to do with the preaching I grew up under. But it's really the other way around. The church is on the offensive. Paul referred to the devil as the god of this world, comparing his rule and reign in the kingdom of darkness to Christ's rule and reign in the kingdom of light. Jesus taught that before one can lay waste to the devil's "house"—the place where the devil rules and reigns—one must tie him up, or "bind the strong man" (Mark 3:27 KJV). The kingdom of God on earth—the church—is continually advancing against the gates of hell, tying up the strong man, plundering his house, and rescuing people out of darkness by the gospel and delivering them into God's kingdom of light.

The Bible tells us that Jesus has the keys of death (Rev. 1:18).

We have the victory because of the finished work of Jesus on the cross. In World War II, between D-Day and V-E Day (victory in Europe day), there was a real battle going on, but the war had already been won on D-Day. In the same way, the cross is D-Day. The war was won at the cross, with the death and resurrection of Jesus. The victory was ours when all the powers of hell could not hold Jesus in the grave and He was raised by the Father's good will. Just as the Allies of World War II knew they had victory when the Germans could not stop them on the beaches of Normandy and Omaha, so was the victory of Jesus when the devil couldn't hold Him in the grave. The second coming of Jesus will be V-E Day, when the whole earth will no longer be under the governance of a dictator. The whole world will be liberated.

In Colossians we see how Jesus made a public spectacle of Satan, triumphing over him through the cross. "When He had disarmed the rulers and authorities, He made a public display of them, having triumphed over them through Him" (Col. 2:15 NASB). Paul was drawing upon the Roman Empire's practice of bringing back to Rome the defeated general of the opposing army. The conquering Roman general riding a white horse or a chariot had the defeated general tied and stripped naked with no signs of authority left. His defeat was a display, a public spectacle before the Roman crowds who came to watch the victory parade. This is the background to understanding Colossians 2:15. This defeated general Satan, tied behind Jesus as He rode His white horse, is the imagery in Colossians. The devil was defeated because of what happened at the cross; all his authority was stripped away. The humiliated, defeated general came back behind Jesus. And because of this victory, Christ in us is the hope of glory.

It's not just about a glorified body, about glory out in the future, in the end times. This glory is also for now. It is a synonym for *power*, the power of the Holy Spirit. The power of the Spirit in you is the hope you have of glory. It is the power by which the signs and wonders of God are displayed for His glory.

When a life that has been shattered by the work of the devil is restored, it brings God glory here and now. There is also a "now and not yet" aspect of Scripture that is at play when God heals.[7] When His power is present in the miraculous, it has an immediate, lifelong, and eternal impact. Let's look at a testimony from Will Hart to better understand what I am talking about. Will is another student in my physical healing course. Like Brian, he was an intern of mine. He was in my first group of interns when I moved to Pennsylvania and started a formal internship program. Now he is the CEO of Iris Global, the ministry in Mozambique, founded by Rolland and Heidi Baker.

I was speaking at a home for troubled youth, at one of their mandatory daily chapel services. There were close to one hundred young people there. I had been told that most came from horrific home circumstances and had been removed for safety issues or legal reasons. Most were not believers. As I was sharing my testimony, I began to feel the presence of the Holy Spirit and began to move in words of knowledge.

During the service I went into a vision as I was calling out people I felt the Lord was highlighting to me. I felt impressed to pray for two girls in particular who were sitting next to each other. As I began to pray and prophesy over the two girls, they both began to weep. I took this as a sign of accuracy and continued to minister. As I began to pray and prophesy about their callings, I went into a vision over one of the girls. I will call her Jane. In the vision, I saw Jane as a small girl, around eight years of age, in a cage with her brother. Both were fully clothed. Jane was wearing sweatpants and a sweatshirt, and so was her brother, who was younger, possibly around five years old. I began to share publicly what I was seeing. I decided to be as specific as I could. I usually would not share something this personal publicly; however, I felt it was necessary because of the environment and that most of the kids in attendance have been abused, and I felt that it was important to be specific.

As the vision continued, the scene with kids in a cage zoomed out where I could see their father with a camera and tripod taking photos of them. I knew that this was for pedophilic purposes. At the same moment, I felt the impression that a doctor had told her that she would have difficulty having children.

I was able to speak directly with Jane afterward. Because the ministry time was with an underaged girl who had suffered abuse, I asked one of the counselors to sit with us. As I asked questions about what I was seeing, she wept and nodded her head. Testing my impressions, especially when dealing with such sensitive information, is so important. I am no stranger to missing words of knowledge. The most important thing is how you share them. Lead with humility and a servant's heart.

Jane confirmed that she and her brother were locked up and held hostage for more than a week. She also confirmed that they were both photographed as young children. Because Jane was around fourteen years old, I felt uncomfortable going into the details of what I saw; however, during our post-prayer time she did confirm that she had medical issues.

At this point, the Holy Spirit was already moving powerfully over Jane. She was shocked by the accuracy and weeping uncontrollably. I felt moved to pray for three things: The first was depression and anger. The second was healing from any physical issues caused by abuse. In my heart, I was praying for her ability to have children; however, I was not praying this out loud. The third prayer was for salvation. I immediately began to pray for more of God's presence. I could visibly see the Holy Spirit moving on her. In this situation, because of the accuracy of the word, all her walls came down. She was fully open to whatever God was saying. My prayer was simply, "More, Lord."

When I asked Jane how she was feeling, she told me that she felt different. She was smiling from ear to ear after I explained to her what happened. She told me nothing like this had ever happened to her before. I don't entirely remember if she said that she no longer had any pain. . . . I asked her about depression, and she pulled up her sleeves and showed me the cut marks on her arms where she tried to take her life. I showed her my arms, where I used to cut as well. Jane said she felt completely different, lighter. I fully believe that she was set free. I asked her if she knew Jesus, and she said she did. I felt like her response was canned, so I encouraged her to go deeper with her faith. She told me she knew Jesus, but whatever just happened was completely different than the Jesus she knew. I encouraged her to read the Bible daily. I also encouraged her that if she ever felt like cutting again that she should just cry out to Jesus, whose body was cut for us.

I believe that God touched Jane that day, and continues to touch her life with His love and His healing so that one day she will walk whole and healed as He intends. And I believe that her testimony and the fruit that is to come from her life will have lasting impact for her and others in this life and the next. Both Will and Jane are experiencing God's kingdom as it comes on the earth now, and both will come into their eternal salvation when the time comes for them to depart this earth to be with Jesus in glory. In the meantime they are actively part of Jesus' prayer that God's kingdom will come "on earth as it is in heaven" (Matt. 6:10).

CHRIST IN YOU

And so this is the mystery, hidden from generations but now revealed to us—Christ in you, the hope of glory! The hope of power! And this hope is not our kind of hope. It's a foundation of certainty. The Greek word for *hope* is stronger than our word for hope *(Strong's 1680)*. The Greek word for *hope* is *elpis*, which means "expectation, trust, confidence, expectation of what is sure or certain." Faith rides on this hope but hope is a foundation of certainty.

Christ in you is the foundation of our certainty that there is going to be a demonstration of power in our lives. The good works that Jesus prepared beforehand are destined for me and for you. I may be saved by grace, but I've been saved to perform and move in the works of God that He prepared for those who are going to be His children (Eph. 2:8–10). So Christ in you, that anointing in you, should be the basis of your hope. You are anointed. The Enemy ought to be afraid of you rather than your being afraid of the Enemy. You are a danger to the devil.

This is why the devil fights against the concept of the priesthood of believers. He does not want us to fully understand that all of us are priests under God—that we're a holy nation, that we all are anointed; that the priesthood is not just for the preachers and apostles and pastors, but Christ in each believer is the hope of glory. Paul doesn't say "Christ in the five-fold ministry is the hope of glory." He said "Christ in you." Jesus didn't say anyone who's an apostle, anyone who's a prophet, anyone who's an evangelist, anyone who's a pastor and teacher would do what He'd been doing, and even greater things. He did not say that. He said in John 14:12 that anyone who believes in Him, greater things than Jesus' miracles shall they do because Jesus was going to the Father.

In the Old Testament, the Spirit did not fall and rest on all God's people, but just on the judges, the kings, the priests, and the prophets. Jesus came to die so that His Spirit could fall on all of us. He didn't come to die just so we can go to heaven. That's wonderful, but that's just one benefit. Jesus came to say, in effect, "I had a plan for a paradise here, and I had a plan for human beings to rule. I had a plan for them to exercise My authority. I had a plan for them, and it got messed up by the Enemy. My people fell, in Adam, but I'm going to reverse that and restore My plan."

The Bible says that in the end times New Jerusalem will come down out of heaven to the earth. We started in paradise and we will end in paradise. And that paradise is here when the lion and the lamb lie down together and the swords are beat into plowshares. That's our hope. Christ in you, the hope of glory, has hope for the future and hope for the present. And as long as people limit their understanding of the gospel to the future, they don't appropriate all that is already theirs in the present. Let's look at the understanding of glory and its relationship to power.

GLORY AND THE MINISTRY OF HEALING

Glory and *power* are often used synonymously in the Bible by John and Paul. We see this in the gospel of John and in the writings of Paul.[8] In the context of the ministry of healing in the church, it is important that we understand the biblical meaning of glory and power, because some reasons given for a lack of healing have to do with a misunderstanding of these terms.

One of the most frequent questions asked about healing is, Why don't more people get healed? No one knows the answer, but there are correlations between what we believe and healing. If we embrace a fundamentalist cessationist theology that says miracles and healings ended when the church was established, or a liberal theology that denies miracles as a possibility not just today but even in the biblical period, we tend to see few, if any, healings. But if we understand the privilege given to us by Christ on the cross, and if we understand how to operate as a priesthood of believers, empowered by the Spirit to do what Jesus did and even greater things than He did, we see more healings. We see God glorified!

Remember the story of the Syrophoenician woman? It's found in both the gospel of Mark (7:25–30) and in Matthew (15:21–28). She's a Gentile. And Jesus had told His followers not to go to the Gentiles but to go into the lost house of Israel until the resurrection, when the power of the Spirit would be poured out. A Syrophoenician woman, a Gentile, came to Jesus and said her daughter needed to be healed—needed to be delivered. Jesus responded by saying something unusual: "It is not right to take the children's bread and toss it to the dogs" (Matt. 15:26). The Jews often referred to Gentiles as dogs, a very derogatory term. Today Jesus would be censured for that. But when Jesus said this to the Syrophoenician woman, He was essentially asking, "How badly do you want this?"

Let's look closer at this passage. When Jesus said, "It's not right to take the children's bread," what did He mean? What is the children's bread in this instance? What did the daughter need? She needed deliverance. Jesus was referring to deliverance as the children's bread. He was saying it was not right to take the children's bread (deliverance ministry) and give it to the dogs, somebody outside the covenant with God. The woman's answer and her faith were stunning. "Yes it is, Lord," she said. "Even the dogs eat the crumbs that fall from their master's table" (v. 27). Jesus, so impressed with her response, and never having seen faith like this, healed her daughter. That which was reserved for the dispensation of the Gentiles, not for the dispensation this woman and her daughter were in, was given to her because of her act of faith. She was able to reach out and bring into her reality something God had reserved for the future. Her faith was so great that she was not willing to embrace an underrealized present reality and so was able to receive in the present what was reserved for the future.

Charles Finney was a man of great faith. He had so much faith for revival that it would break out in churches when he visited, even in those churches that had been praying and praying for revival but had not seen it until he came. Even though they had prayed for revival, they had not had faith for it to come, and it did not come. It is important to understand that great faith is not "the answer" in the ministry of healing unless that great faith is accompanied by an expectation (a focus) and an understanding that healing is not to be a rare exception but the natural display of God's glory. Finney had great faith for revival but little faith for healing. His historical context placed him in a time when Protestantism did not teach that gifts of healing were for today. His theology was undermining his faith—not in regard to revival or salvation but in regard to healing.

The same applies to healings, miracles, signs, and wonders. We can be strong in faith and yet not see healing because we need to have faith *for healing*. We need to understand that the anointing can bubble up in us even when we are not yet strong in faith because the One inside of us (Jesus) has great faith. And sometimes when that bubbling up happens we still tend to doubt, wondering and questioning if it's really God. We get into wrestling matches, battles in which our little faith tries to pull down the faith of Christ in us. My advice is to forget the battle and just go with Jesus. He is in us, and He is mighty to save.

SOVEREIGNTY, HOLINESS, AND POWER IN THE MINISTRY OF HEALING

Some attribute a lack of healings to the sovereignty of God,[9] that what does and doesn't happen in regard to healing is due to the sovereignty of God, placing little emphasis upon the understanding and expectant faith of the one in need of healing or the one praying for healing. But I think an overemphasis on sovereignty is an insufficient explanation. There are also other reasons. People with great healing anointings see more healings than others, which indicates to me that it is not just sovereignty at play in healing.

In the 1800s, when the Protestant church began to recapture the understanding that healing is in the promises of God and part of the benefits of the atonement, they began to see more healings than Protestant churches had seen up to that point. I believe that it is more the will of God to heal than the doctrine of the sovereignty of God would lead us to believe or, rather, doubt. And it is a richer, fuller understanding of the atonement, an understanding of the cross, which allows us to recapture the biblical basis for healing. Maria Woodworth-Etter, John G. Lake, Smith Wigglesworth, Oral Roberts, and others who believed in healings saw more healings than ministers who didn't believe healing was for today or provided for in the atonement. It wasn't sovereignty that determined the numbers of healings; it was what people believed that determined the numbers of healings they saw in their meetings. Not that sovereignty was never part of the answer; it was just overemphasized.

I believe that sometimes, in His sovereignty, God doesn't heal. There is a tension that exists, but does sovereignty have to make God a grinch? I don't think so. We have just overused sovereignty to the point that we end up portraying God as tight-fisted, as a God who is hard to get anything out of. But it's the other way around—we have a God who loves to give good gifts to His children, a God who sent His Son to die on the cross where He bore our sicknesses and diseases, a God who moves in power to heal through the finished work of Christ on the cross. We have a God who revealed Himself and His attitude toward healing in His Son, Jesus.

A misunderstanding of holiness also helped erect another barrier to the flow of healing in the church, especially the Catholic Church. Holiness in the Catholic Church was relegated to the domain of the priests, monks, and nuns who were deemed the only ones "holy enough" to minister healing. This was much more the case before the 1960s than after Vatican Council II, and the Catholic Charismatic Renewal, which began in 1967. Before the 1960s the church believed that lay persons would not be used by God because they lacked the necessary commitment displayed by the clergy.

This concept of holiness or lack of holiness was taken to its extreme in the Middle Ages when lay persons who moved in the gift of prophecy or words of knowledge could be burned at the stake as witches. At this point in history, the church understood that the occult had power, and from that understanding came the belief that anyone displaying power who was not a "holy" priest, monk, or nun must be displaying the power to predict, prophesy, or heal by the power of the devil. Eddie Hyatt, in his book *2,000 Years of Charismatic Christianity*, revealed that for two thousand years this argument that attributes the power of God to the devil has been used against renewal movements in the church as almost the singular strategy of Satan. Enthusiasm, fanaticism, rejecting manifestations often as of the devil, along with a lack of morality and the institutionalization of the charismata in the bishops, led to conflict between the bishops (later in the church) and the charismatically endowed.[10] I call this the Beelzebub controversy, alluding to the Pharisees attributing Jesus' power to heal and cast out demons to Beelzebub, the prince of demons.

The Catholic Church, during a significant portion of its history—especially the Middle Ages—believed demonstrations of miracles, signs, and wonders flowed only from the saintly, the holy. The miracles of the saintly led to the canonization of saints. Now the laity were instructed to pray to the saints who would then work miracles for them. It became a double bind. People did not believe that their prayers for healing (or for someone else's healing) would be heard because they were not holy enough, and so they didn't pray for healing. This is the strategy of the Enemy to keep us from understanding that God can use us, that Christ in us is the hope of glory. Thankfully, this is not the current position of the Roman Catholic Church. With the influence of the Charismatic Renewal[11] and healthy theological dialogue on the issues related to the Holy Spirit and His gifts, there is now a much healthier perspective on healing within Catholicism. Likewise, we are seeing growing improvement in the percentage of Protestants who now believe in healing and believe that such healing can occur through the laity, not just the clergy.

Some seem to think healings don't occur because God runs out of power. Have you ever heard anyone say, "Well, I'd like to be healed, but this person's need is so much greater than mine that I don't want you to pray for me because this person has a terminal illness, and I've just got this little problem." In other words, they think God's going to run out of power. He's going to go broke at some point. What kind of a God are we thinking about who doesn't have enough power to heal everyone?

Our God is all sufficient. He does not run out of power, nor does He run out of grace. In the next chapter we will examine what it means to live in the world with persevering grace that comes from the anointing of the Holy Spirit. We are the people of God, whom Christ indwells. When we understand the fullness of who He is, we can live with freedom and boldness to see His kingdom come, His will done on earth as it is in heaven.

NINE

PERSECUTION, TRIBULATION, AND GLORY

THE INDWELLING OF THE HOLY SPIRIT WILL OFTEN
determine whether one remains faithful to Jesus or commits apostasy in time of severe persecution or tribulation. Often during such times the glory of God is seen among His people. And as a result of their faithfulness in suffering, they receive a greater glory.[1] In Scripture we find tribulation in two different contexts. One is the Great Tribulation Jesus speaks of in the Olivet Discourse in Matthew 24 and 25, Mark 13, and Luke 21, which will occur at the end of the age, when Jesus returns. We also find tribulation in Scripture referring to times of great suffering and hardship. In the eighteenth century, in response to the severe anti-Catholic sentiment prevalent at the time, a French Jesuit priest, Manual Lucanza, penned a three-volume book that would contribute to a new teaching in the church in America.[2] This new teaching contributed to what became dispensational pre-tribulation rapture, premillennial eschatology. It cannot be found in the history of the church as an

accepted teaching by Protestants before 1830. John Nelson Darby was the major contributor to this new way of interpreting the Bible. Scofield included it in the notes of his Scofield Bible and it became *the* major view of the church. Many Protestant churches in America boldly proclaim a "come to Jesus and get saved and you won't have to go through the tribulation" message. While there is comfort to be found in pre-tribulation, premillennial eschatology, it leaves believers unprepared when life's inevitable tribulations do come. This pre-tribulation, pre-millennial eschatology had been taught to the Chinese people by American missionaries. Many fell away from the Lord, or at least denied the Lord, when persecution did come, especially during the Cultural Revolution in China; their faith hadn't prepared them for tribulation. Those who were able to persevere became filled with the Spirit. During this time of great persecution, when it was difficult to gain access to the whole Bible, the book of Acts was their most prized portion of Scripture.

Why should we be the only part of the church that never has to go through any tribulation? In the entire world today there are more Christians in the last hundred years who have died for the faith than in the first three hundred years of the church. What we need is Christ in us, the hope of glory. We need the fullness of the Holy Spirit in order to be faithful to God if we have to be tried. We need the reality of Christ in us, the hope of glory, so we don't buckle when all hell breaks loose against us and when persecution comes against us. We need persevering grace because of the anointing of the Spirit upon us.

My friends Rolland and Heidi Baker live and walk daily in the reality of Christ in us with a persevering grace that moves me to tears. Married in 1980, they left for Indonesia as missionaries two weeks after they married with one-way tickets and just a few dollars in their pockets. Rolland came from a family of missionaries. Brilliant and on fire for God, he gave up a scholarship and a career in science to pursue God instead, majoring in biblical studies. Heidi grew up in Laguna Beach, California, living a privileged life until one summer when God touched her with the fire of His Holy Spirit and changed her into a radical lover of Jesus whose only aim in life became to love the Lord and serve Him. Together the couple embarked on a journey that now spans forty years. From day one they were drawn to serve the poorest of the poor. They have lived in the dirt, faced hunger and death, been beaten too many times to count, been driven from countries they were serving, been persecuted by governments, and seen years of hard work washed away by cyclones. Through it all, they have remained steadfast to God's call on their lives to serve the poor. Their ministry, Iris Global,[3] provides both humanitarian aid and spiritual aid through the gospel of Jesus Christ. In 2019 they distributed 4,957 Bible materials, ministered to 3,650 people in prisons, reached 114,535 people through their community outreach programs, operated 9 mission schools with 537 students attending, had 12,604 people in discipleship groups, and trained 3,597 people to minister to others. They feed thousands daily, have sponsorship programs for children, offer community programs to strengthen families, and provide K-12 education to more than a thousand children a year. They plan to soon open Iris University in Mozambique, fully accredited by the government, to educate future leaders. These leaders can then help by serving in existing ministries of Iris Global that respond to cyclones with relief efforts, build homes, drill wells, run more than a dozen indigenous farm and agriculture projects, run more than a dozen micro-enterprise initiatives, and treat everyone who comes to them in hospital outreaches and local clinics. If that weren't enough, Iris

Global has a school of the arts in Los Angeles founded to impact this generation to release the kingdom through media and arts. I could go on, but I urge you to further explore what God is doing through the Bakers and Iris Global.

The Bakers are currently living in a city in Mozambique where a very high percentage of its population are refugees, many of whom are recent converts to Christianity. They have escaped radical militia of another faith who have burned their homes and decapitated many pastors and key leaders of the new churches. These militia are close to the city in which Rolland and Heidi live. Yet, though encouraged by many to leave the city, they are staying, knowing that it could be overrun by the rebels and they would be key targets. This is the persevering grace that brings about unnatural courage. Like Paul, the Bakers can say they are willing to spend and be spent for the salvation of others' souls (2 Cor. 12:15).

UNDERSTANDING WHO
WE ARE IN CHRIST

We need to come into the fullness of the understanding that we have something greater in us than outward holiness. We have the anointing of the Holy Spirit *in* our lives. And we don't have to be perfect to be used by God, because the perfect One [Christ] who lives in us is the One who can use us. We need to *believe* that Christ in us is the hope of glory. And this glory is not just for the future, when we die. It is for the future *and* for now. The Lord's Prayer is in part a warfare prayer. When Jesus tells us to pray, "Our Father who art in heaven, hallowed be thy name, thy kingdom come, thy will be done, on earth as it is in heaven," He is teaching us to pray for the kingdom of God to come against the kingdom of this world (Matt. 6:9–10 RSV). This warfare prayer is His desire. Instead of praying that we can get out of the earth and into heaven, we should be praying that heaven comes to earth in us, because the power of heaven is in us through the finished work of Jesus Christ on the cross—and it defeats the Enemy. Here is a recent testimony from Nigeria to illustrate the power of Christ over all other powers. It also illustrates the importance and the ability to hear communications from God.

In the early 1900s a mainline denomination church was established in a small town in Nigeria. Fast-forward—one of the local leaders of that church had a teenage daughter, Sophia Odunlami, a lovely young woman who taught school in the town. Sophia and many others were hit by an epidemic. Sophia lay ill at home. After five days of suffering, she had an encounter with God in which He directed her to tell the people that they should believe that only God has power over the epidemic, and if they would wash in a coming rainfall they would be healed. Sophia shared this message with her father and the local pastor. News of this incident spread quickly.

Sophia then began to warn the people to refrain from idolatry and charms and trust God only. She was invited to share with a group at the local church, and when she addressed them one Sunday evening, she reiterated God's message that a rain would soon fall and it should be used with faith for healing. Sure enough, the rain came, and all who used the rain praised its effectiveness to heal. Then trouble broke out against Sophia and her father in their hometown and from the mainline denomination church in town. After repeated attempts on her life and unbearable suffering and persecution, Sophia decided to move. Meanwhile, the local church had been shut down because of the epidemic, and the local pastor had returned to his village in accordance with government directives. Church members saw the pastor's departure as desertion.

When Sophia returned to speak, a group within the church felt inspired by her message and "led a procession of church members about the town praying for deliverance from the epidemic." The result of the healings that followed convinced them that the promises of the Bible, especially in the New Testament, had contemporary meaning. This was the origin of the preaching and practice of divine healing in Southern Nigeria on a major scale.[4]

The power of God defeated demonic powers that wanted to kill via an epidemic and wanted to shut down the move of God to heal and raise up Sophia and her father to be used to start a divine healing movement in Nigeria. Much fruit has since flowed from God's move upon the church in Nigeria. The following story of the power of the Holy Spirit over all other powers is from sixth-century—almost seventh-century—Kent, England. It is an amazing testimony to the power of the gospel when it is accompanied by signs and wonders and how often this is the reason for entire people groups coming to Christ.

In AD 595 Pope Gregory sent Augustine (not to be confused with Saint Augustine of Hippo), prior of the Abbey of Saint Andrew's in Rome, to Kent, England, to convert the Anglo-Saxons to

Christianity. These Anglo-Saxons were composed of pagan tribes, among them the Picts and the Druids, which were demonized people groups. This mission, known as the Gregorian Mission, was quite successful, with Augustine baptizing 10,000 one Christmas Day, much like the mass baptisms of New Testament times. Pope Gregory the Great, who sent him to Kent, said this about his apostolic mission, "But, since in the good things you do I know that you also rejoice with others, I make you a return for your favor, and announce things not unlike yours; for while the nation of the Angli, placed in a corner of the world, remained up to this time misbelieving in the worship of sticks and stones, I determined, through the aid of your prayers for me, to send to it, God granting it, a monk of my monastery for the purpose of preaching. And he, having with my leave been made bishop by the bishops of Germany, proceeded, with their aid also, to the end of the world to the aforesaid nation; and already letters have reached us telling us of his safety and his work; to the effect that he and those that have been sent with him are resplendent with such great miracles in the said nation that they seem to imitate the powers of the apostles in the signs which they display. Moreover, at the solemnity of the Lord's Nativity which occurred in this first indiction, more than ten thousand Angli are reported to have been baptized by the same our brother and fellow bishop.[5]

Augustine was successful not because of good preaching or teaching but because the power of God was demonstrated to be greater than the power of the occult. This power of God that accompanied the preaching of the gospel is what caused them to believe in the gospel. Being saved from the powers of the demonic and from disease caused them to believe. Believing in the power of the gospel preceded believing that the Bible was God's Word. These pagan people groups practiced witchcraft and magic, and they understood the significance and power of occult spells and curses. In the occult realm, if someone works a pact or a covenant that has power to bring you into bondage, you must then find a more powerful witch or warlock who can work a more powerful pact in order to break the pact or covenant. You can be freed from one bondage only to come under a stronger bondage. It's all about who has the most power.

The new covenant in the blood of Jesus is more powerful than any other pact or covenant. When these pagan people groups were confronted with the power of God in Christ Jesus, they converted by the thousands. In the Gospels we see the power and authority of Jesus over the demonic realm.

> Just then a man in their synagogue who was possessed by an impure spirit cried out, "What do you want with us, Jesus of Nazareth? Have you come to destroy us? I know who you are— the Holy One of God!"
>
> "Be quiet!" said Jesus sternly. "Come out of him!" The impure spirit shook the man violently and came out of him with a shriek.
>
> The people were all so amazed that they asked each other, "What is this? A new teaching—and with authority! He even gives orders to impure spirits and they obey him." (Mark 1:23–27)

In Mark 1:34 and again in Mark 3:11–12 we see Jesus addressing the demons and forbidding them to give witness to who He was. The ancient Eastern Aramaic translation of Mark 1:34 says that Jesus would not allow the demons to speak "because some of them were his acquaintances." Before Satan and his demons were cast out of heaven, they were in fellowship with Jesus while they were still angels. The demons submit to Jesus' authority because they know Him as the Holy One of God, the Son of God. They know who He is!

"Whenever the impure spirits saw him, they fell down before him and cried out, 'You are the Son of God.' But he gave them strict orders not to tell others about him" (Mark 3:11–12).

DESTINED FOR GLORY

If the demons know and understand the power and authority of Jesus, should not we, His people, also understand who He is and live in the reality of the privilege given to us through His finished work on the cross? We have been given privilege, and we must recover our emphasis on our privilege, who we are—that we are a people of faith, and we have faith that the Spirit in us is the hope of glory. All Christians have the anointing of Christ within them. We are loaded for ministry, loaded for glory, and destined for glory. I believe it is the Lord's will for His people to understand that destiny. Ours is not a destiny of defeat and shame but a destiny of glory. Jesus wants us to bear much fruit and to see much glory. In John 14 to 16, when Jesus talks about fruit, He is talking about asking the Father for things, and He tells the disciples, "whoever believes in me will do the works I have been doing, and they will do even greater things than these, because I am going to the Father. And I will do whatever you ask in my name, so that the Father may be glorified in the Son" (John 14:12–13). Jesus wants us to bring glory to His Father by what we do.[6]

We are to co-labor with Christ. "For we are God's fellow workers. You are God's field, God's building" (1 Cor. 3:9 ESV). Co-laboring with God is not something we do of ourselves. We are not channeling energy. We are fellow workers with the Holy Spirit, with God through the Holy Spirit. When we minister, we are to minister with the energy of God, the power of God. This is the will of God. It is our inheritance and our destiny. We need to meditate upon 2 Corinthians 4:13 and John 16:15 until these scriptures take root in us.

> It is written: "I believed; therefore I have spoken." With that same spirit of faith we also believe and therefore speak. (2 Cor. 4:13)

> "All that belongs to the Father is mine. That is why I said the Spirit will receive from me what he will make known to you." (John 16:15)

It is the revelation that comes out of relationship that gives us the faith to seek what we think God is saying in any given situation. And this is where the finished work of Christ on the cross comes into its proper position. We can now boldly approach the throne of grace in our time of need because of what Jesus has already done.[7] We are seated with Christ in heavenly places.[8] He has given us authority. We are to boldly come on the basis of what He did, not our own performance. That access to the throne room is the key to our understanding of the finished work of the cross. He has made each of us holy. But to keep this in balance, we need to work out that salvation with fear and trembling.[9] It is by grace, but we have the responsibility to walk in relationship with Him, working out all that this relationship means. This isn't always easy, as the following testimony from Jessika Tate, another one of my physical healing course students, illustrates. She is a consultant to the largest traditional Baptist church in Brazil with an average weekly attendance of eighteen thousand. We have hosted several healing schools in this church and had some of its key leaders come to our headquarters for our Global Summer Intensive that runs for three weeks. Jessika remembers:

As I was waiting for my turn to speak in a workshop, I began to feel itching on my skin. This wasn't just a normal, centralized itch; it felt like a painful sensation all down my arms and legs. It had come so suddenly and intensely that I immediately knew it must be a word of knowledge. To be honest, I didn't think this was the best type of setting to go after healing. I had been given a specific topic to speak on, and I had a very defined and limited time frame. With the limitations and nature of the workshop, I was a little nervous because I knew I would be going against the grain. It is difficult to communicate how little I wanted to give this word of knowledge. Originally when I felt it I was thinking, *How can I get out of giving this word from the stage?* The setting did not feel appropriate. There were several senior leaders of our movement and visiting pastors, and it was meant to be a teaching workshop. On top of that, I was thinking, *A RASH? You want me to break the flow for a rash!* To put it lightly, I did not have the best attitude.

I wrapped up a few minutes early and gave the word of knowledge for someone with a skin condition that caused itching and burning. In order not to disrupt the workshop, I asked

147

whoever that might be to meet me in the back of the room. One young woman came over and she was crying before she even got to me. One look at her skin and I saw it was covered in red spots, open wounds, and severe dry patches as well.

When the girl walked toward me and I could see the severity of her skin condition, as well as the pain in her eyes, my heart just broke. I am not certain if it was more for her pain or remorse over my bad attitude. It reminds me of a time that one of my heroes, Corrie Ten Boom, was in Colombia ministering and said that she hoped no one responded to the altar call because she was hot, tired, and wanted to go home.[10]

My heart was so moved with compassion when the girl came up that I asked if I could hug her. She nodded yes, and I pulled her into an embrace. As I held her, I asked what her name was and asked how long she had had the condition. She told me that she had the condition since she was born. At this point we came out of the embrace, and I began to interview her. I asked her to describe what she felt in her body in that moment. She said that her skin always itches at least somewhere on her body, it is often accompanied with burning, which results in her scratching and having open sores almost constantly. I asked how much of her body it covered. She said almost all of it, but predominantly her arms, legs, and scalp. She showed me the sores on her legs and on her scalp. They were red and ranged in size from the smudge of a pencil eraser up to about a half-dollar size. I asked what her pain level was. She said at the moment it was only about five, but depending on the day it stays between a two and up to a ten. As we were speaking my heart was feeling heavier and heavier. I've noticed that after I went through PTSD myself, I normally can "feel" if someone is battling a suicidal spirit or any form of anxiety or depression. This also tends to be an area I see great breakthrough in. I asked if she had been dealing with depression and she began to weep.

It was clear that before I ministered physical healing that she needed inner healing. Usually in conditions that began at birth or have been long-term conditions, there is good reason to suspect an afflicting spirit, and I've found that also to be true with depression. I was about to move forward with that issue when I heard the Holy Spirit say, *Tell her that she is beautiful.* I looked her in the eyes and I said to her in Portuguese, *"Você é linda."* When I said this she doubled over and began wailing.

I asked the Holy Spirit to come, and I moved to a commanding prayer to tell the spirits to leave. I started with telling the spirit of self-hatred to leave and then also the spirit of depression. As Doris Wagner says, "roots produce fruit," so I went through a few of the spirits that typically seem to partner with issues of rejection, self-hatred, and so on. While I was commanding the spirits to leave, she remained bent over and crying. It was obvious something was happening in her, so I began to pray in tongues until I knew what to do next.

When she stood upright, I asked how she was feeling. She said that she felt lighter, she felt peace, and that she could feel joy for the first time in a very long time. I did not feel like my time with her was done as she still had her skin condition. I asked if it was okay if we continued. She said that it was. Knowing that she had dealt with rejection and self-hatred, I wanted to take a few minutes to deal with ways she had cursed herself. The Global Awakening Ministry Team Training Manual[11] mentions that when people curse themselves it gives the demonic access to their lives. I took a moment to explain to her about self-curses and what they can do. I then asked if she had verbally cursed herself. She said that she had. I told her that if she was willing we were going to take a minute to ask for forgiveness for that and then move to praying for her condition. She agreed, and I led her in a few prayers to ask forgiveness for cursing herself. Then I still wanted to pray for her skin condition as it had not changed. I asked her if I could put my hands on her arms where some of her skin had open abrasions, and she said I could.

The moment was feeling very tender, and so I again asked if the Holy Spirit would come and touch her body as He had touched her heart. When I asked Him to do this, I began to feel His presence. It wasn't heat or electricity but an extreme level of tangible peace. She and my translator were crying and, to be honest, I was too. His presence was strong. I did not ask God to heal her, but I looked down at her arms, and places that were red had returned back to normal. I continued to pray softly in tongues, and little by little we watched as her arms returned to normal. After a few minutes my translator just looked at me in shock and said, "Her skin is clear!" Where she had been covered in sores and red welts there only remained one tiny little red dot about the size of my pinkie fingernail.

We all should be walking in the revelation that comes out of relationship with God, as Jessika Tate and many others have learned to do, which gives us the faith to seek what we think He is saying in any given situation. My desire is to experience Him and to see myself as He says I am. I want to become so free that I can do everything that He wants and can confess what He says about me. That is the freedom I am looking for. That is what I believe the finished work is—a boldness to come on the basis of what He did, not abusing His teaching or removing everything else that Scripture teaches about the importance of utilizing our Advocate. I am not talking about a license to sin. I am talking about living in the finished work of Christ on the cross, living with boldness in this reality. Yet, as important as it is to know who I am in Christ, it is also important to know who Christ is in me: the hope of glory. A lack of understanding on either side of this equation is detrimental to our ability to be powerfully used of God.

TEN

HOW GOD REVEALS HIS GLORY

THE RELATIONSHIP OF GLORY TO HEALINGS AND
miracles can be found in both the Old Testament as seen in the
Law and the Prophets, and in the New Testament as seen in
the Gospels. Let us first look at this relationship as it is found
in the Old Testament. One of the ways God reveals His glory is
through His provision.

In Exodus 16:4–6, we see God's miraculous provision for the
Israelites. In this passage, as Moses and Aaron admonish the Israelites
for their ungrateful grumbling against the Lord, the people look
toward the desert and see the glory of the Lord appear in a cloud
(v. 10).

> "The LORD said to Moses, 'I have heard the grumbling of the
> Israelites. Tell them, "At twilight you will eat meat, and in the
> morning you will be filled with bread. Then you will know that
> I am the LORD your God.'" That evening quail came and covered

the camp, and in the morning there was a layer of dew around the camp. When the dew was gone, thin flakes like frost on the ground appeared on the desert floor." (Ex. 16:11–14)

Moses told the Israelites that they would see God's glory in the morning, in His provision of bread (manna) to eat, and they did. Six mornings each week for forty years manna appeared on the ground to feed them. That miraculous provision was a manifestation of God's glory. God not only gave them bread to eat, but He gave them water to drink.

> Moses and Aaron went from the assembly to the entrance to the tent of meeting and fell facedown, and the glory of the LORD appeared to them. The LORD said to Moses, "Take the staff, and you and your brother Aaron gather the assembly together. Speak to that rock before their eyes and it will pour out its water. You will bring water out of the rock for the community so they and their livestock can drink."
>
> So Moses took the staff from the LORD's presence, just as he commanded him. He and Aaron gathered the assembly together in front of the rock and Moses said to them, "Listen, you rebels, must we bring you water out of this rock?" Then Moses raised his arm and struck the rock twice with his staff. Water gushed out, and the community and their livestock drank. (Num. 20:6–11)

In the Old Testament we see God's compassion followed by demonstrations of His power. This is a reflection of God's true character. He is a God of mercy and compassion, and He desires to touch His people. When we ask for the compassion of God, we will receive it. For God to do otherwise would be cruel and outside of His nature. Lamentations 3:23 says that God's mercies are new every morning, and great is His faithfulness. I am constantly touched by the unfailing faithfulness and mercy of God as I see and hear time and again how much He cares for each one of us. This testimony from Brian Starley beautifully illustrates the lengths God will go to in order to touch one person.

As I was getting close to my home, I passed a man on the street. He was sitting on the curbside next to the gas station. When I passed by him, he said, "Hey, would you be able to spot me twenty dollars?" I didn't have any cash on me, and before I could say anything, the Holy Spirit instantly took my mind to Peter's interaction with the lame man outside the gate beautiful. Along with this thought, I heard the phrase *patellar fracture*. I asked the man his name and then introduced myself. "Brian, I'm a Christian and sometimes God will speak to me about others, and it's often to do with physical healing. I think He's telling me that you have a patellar fracture, and He wants to heal you." He immediately looked stunned and responded with, "Wow! That's crazy . . . I don't have that, but my friend does; he's staying with me a few blocks that way. Do you want to come and tell him that?"

This response was shocking for a few reasons. First, I was surprised to find out that the word wasn't for him and amazed that God would orchestrate the events for me to reach his friend. Second, I was taken back by his instantaneous excitement and readiness for me to come and tell his friend. John Wimber teaches that encounters overcome the obstacle of unbelief. I believe that is exactly what happened here; the word of knowledge created the capacity for Brian's friend Matt to believe that it was God. I agreed to follow him to his house, although we were heading toward a very dangerous part of town. Despite this, I knew it was the Lord and have seen His track record of consistently showing up and being with me.

We reached his home in a few minutes, and Brian led me upstairs to his friend, who was sitting on their couch. He was obviously very surprised to see me there, and Brian quickly explained why I was in the house. I introduced myself to Matt and relayed what God had spoken to me. He was stunned and pointed over to a pair of crutches propped against the wall. He told me, "That's exactly right. I was in a car accident, and I had multiple injuries to my legs, the worst being my broken right kneecap." I asked Matt if I could pray for his leg to be healed and he agreed. I decided upon a commanding prayer, speaking to his leg and kneecap to be restored. I began by praying, "Come, Holy Spirit, and touch Matt. I command the knee and all areas affected in his leg to be healed. In the name of Jesus, I declare healing and wholeness to him now." Due to the circumstances and the accuracy of the word of knowledge, my faith was very high. I had a strong inner assurance that God was going to heal Matt's leg. After praying only a short amount of time, he interrupted me and said that he felt heat coming all over his entire body.

I then stopped praying and asked him if he would be willing to test it out; I explained that we often see the body healed as the person tries to do what they usually cannot. He started by reaching down and feeling his knee; then he looked up at me with tears in his eyes as he said, "It feels totally different!" Then, he stood up on his own without the crutches and without me helping him. He began bending down and putting pressure on his leg in several ways, then discovered that he had been completely healed.

I have found that what works best for me in these moments is to say something like, "I didn't do this to you; it was Jesus. And what Jesus just did for your body is what He wants to give you in every area of your life. Do you want to know Him?" So I asked Matt, and he said yes as he cried. Brian was shocked at everything happening, and he, too, wanted to know Jesus. I then prayed with them both, leading them to Jesus and praying that the Holy Spirit would fill them. Brian did not have any visible manifestations, but Matt's body shook when I prayed for the Spirit's infilling upon his life.

I was deeply touched by what happened, and I thanked them for letting me come and pray for them. I encouraged both of them to begin going to church. I ended our time together by encouraging them to share what happened with each of their other housemates and others they meet.

HIS GLORY REVEALED IN MINISTRY TO THE POOR

The prophet Isaiah tells us that when we minister to the poor, God's glory will be revealed.

"Is not this the kind of fasting I have chosen:
to loose the chains of injustice

and untie the cords of the yoke,
to set the oppressed free
and break every yoke?
Is it not to share your food with the hungry
and to provide the poor wanderer with shelter—
when you see the naked, to clothe them,
and not to turn away from your own flesh and blood?
Then your light will break forth like the dawn,
and your healing will quickly appear;
then your righteousness will go before you,
and the glory of the LORD will be your rear guard.
Then you will call, and the LORD will answer;
you will cry for help, and he will say: Here am I.

"If you do away with the yoke of oppression,
with the pointing finger and malicious talk,
and if you spend yourselves in behalf of the hungry
and satisfy the needs of the oppressed,
then your light will rise in the darkness,
and your night will become like the noonday.
The LORD will guide you always;
he will satisfy your needs in a sun-scorched land
and will strengthen your frame.
You will be like a well-watered garden,
like a spring whose waters never fail.
Your people will rebuild the ancient ruins
and will raise up the age-old foundations;
you will be called Repairer of Broken Walls,
Restorer of Streets with Dwellings."

(ISA. 58:6–12)

If we will spend ourselves on behalf of the poor, feeding the hungry, clothing the naked, and sheltering the homeless, God says that our light will rise in the darkness and our night will become like noonday. His glory will be revealed through us as we minister in His name.

In the New Testament, under the new covenant, God's compassion is followed by demonstrations of His power through healings, miracles, signs, and wonders. These things are expressions of the gospel. Healings, miracles, signs, and wonders do not just testify to the gospel but are an integral part of it. God the Father and the Son are glorified through miracles and healings.

I emphasize healings and miracles because I want God to receive glory. I don't just want to see His glory; I want Him to receive glory. The life and ministry of Jesus were all about the Father receiving glory. And we are to continue the ministry of Jesus in the power of the Holy Spirit, giving glory to God. It is not a selfish thing to ask for the glory of God. It is not a selfish thing to ask to see people healed. Some people say healing ministry does seem selfish to them; they think it is all focused on the ministry team. No! It is not about us; it is about Him. He wants to receive glory. During the Azusa Street Revival, they would tell people that God wanted to show His glory; God wanted to do something to reveal His glory. They believed that the outpouring of the Spirit was to bring glory to God. I believe that too.

When we sing the words, "Glorify Thy name, glorify Thy name, glorify Thy name in all the earth," do we understand what we are asking God to do? From a biblical perspective we are literally asking God to do just that—glorify His name. But a lot of us in the church don't have faith that He is going to actually show His glory. I would like to see us, the church, sing from our hearts with an expectation that says, "God, we really do want You to receive glory. We really do want to see You glorify Your name!"

In our work with the poor in St. Louis and with Rolland and Heidi Baker in Mozambique, we have seen that when our expectation for God to reveal His glory is high, we see Him move in glory. In the 1990s, when I pastored a church in St. Louis, we would go into the inner city, into the projects, with food. We didn't want to just donate food to a food bank (donating is a good thing, by the way). We wanted to take the food to the people ourselves so we would have opportunities to minister to them. Some people told us it was too risky, but we never felt unsafe and we made friends with the people we ministered to. In the privacy of their federal housing apartments, they would open up to us, disclosing their problems, and we would pray for them. Members of our church saw more miracles take place among the poor in St. Louis than anywhere else. The light of Christ rose in us in the midst of the darkness and shone like noonday. God showed His glory.

"THIS WILL NOT DO!"

Once when I was ministering in South Carolina, oppression came over the meeting. There were almost four hundred people present, but only four were healed despite many words of knowledge. I felt anger rising in me, and I stood up and said, "This will not do! This is not good enough! God does not get glory when only four people out of four hundred are healed. I am expectant for at least 10 percent of you to be healed tonight. We cannot quit. We have to press through this. We're going for it!" At that point more words of knowledge came forth and faith began to rise. As we prayed, people began to get healed. Before the night was over we had eighty people healed. Understand, I was thankful for the four people who were healed, but I knew that what was happening was not worthy of God.

I want to challenge every one of you, especially every pastor reading this, and ask, "How concerned are you for the glory of God?" Pastors, hear me: It's not about how good our sermons are. It's not about how beautiful the sanctuary is, how beautiful the décor is. It is about the glory of God. We ought to be concerned about the ways in which God gets glory. I keep coming back to this point because there are too many who do not understand this. I'm not talking about a selfish thing here. This is a Christ-centered issue. This is what Jesus died for. This is why the Holy Spirit was poured out.

Jesus died on the cross, poured out the Holy Spirit, and gave us gifts because He wants the Father to receive glory and the Father wants to glorify the Son. And when we have a service and nobody gets healed and there are no miracles, we may be having a good service from our perspective, but I believe heaven weeps. I believe it grieves the heart of God when we have a service and people are present who are in need of healing but there are no healings—no miracles. Something is missing when the glory of God is not in the house of God. God wants the glory to be in the church and, outside the walls of the church, in us who are the church. The problem is not on His part: the problem is on our part because we do not understand. "Where there is no vision, the people perish" (Prov. 29:18 KJV).

There is biblical revelation for this in the story of Jesus changing the water to wine, which we discussed earlier, as found in the gospel of John. "What Jesus did here in Cana of Galilee was the first of the signs through which he revealed his glory; and his disciples believed in him" (John 2:11). When we have a service with no healings, Jesus is not able to reveal His glory. There are no miracles taking place because we have become a "Nazareth," a culture of unbelief —skeptical—like Nazareth where Jesus, because of their unbelief, did not do any mighty deeds except heal a few. And we're not going to see disciples put their faith in God when this happens. But when we have a service where the glory of God is revealed in the miraculous, we will see an increase in faith.

During the Azusa Street Revival (1906 in Los Angeles, California, the birthplace of a great Pentecostal revival), there were so many healings taking place that one could not help but begin to believe for miracles. People were given faith by being in an atmosphere where the miraculous was happening. We need to contend for the glory of God to be revealed in our churches through miracles and healings so that the name of Jesus will be held in high honor and He will receive the glory due Him. When this happens, those sitting in the pews will put their faith in Him.

We have too many people in church who are not putting their faith in God because they have not yet seen His glory revealed. We can scold them and tell them they need to have more faith, but how are they to get that faith? In his letter to the church in Rome, Paul tells believers that "faith comes from hearing, and hearing through the word of Christ" (Rom. 10:17 ESV). In Ephesians, he says that faith is a gift, given to believers by the Holy Spirit.[1] Faithfulness is seen as a fruit of the Spirit in Galatians.[2] I believe faith also comes when we say, "God, reveal Your glory! Manifest Your presence! Heal the sick; perform miracles!" When we contend in this way, faith is going to come, but it's got to start somewhere. It only takes a handful of people contending in faith for it to come. Then the rest will follow.

Evangelist Mel Tari wrote a book titled *Like a Mighty Wind*, chronicling the revival that swept the island of Timor in 1965.[3] So powerful was this revival that the mighty wind of God continues to blow through Indonesia today. Some years after the publication of this book, Mel was criticized for exaggerating what really happened during the revival. The stories were so amazing that some readers were having a hard time believing them. The truth is that Mel watered down the stories because he knew that many in the Western church would not believe what God had done. He knew that if he told the full extent of what God had done, many would write him off as crazy and never read anything about this mighty move. How sad.

REVELATION PRODUCES FAITH TO DO THE WORKS OF THE FATHER TO HIS GLORY

When I talk about the concept of glorification, I'm referring to the revelation and faith to do the works of God. The Father's glorification of Jesus is implied—that He was glorified by the words and the works the Father gave Him to do. Jesus was glorified not just with words to speak to people but also with words of instruction about what to do, with the revelation that creates the faith that produces the miraculous.

Jesus said, "If I glorify myself, my glory means nothing. My Father, whom you claim as your God, is the one who glorifies me" (John 8:54). When Jesus heard the report that Lazarus was sick, Jesus was looking forward to a miracle. He said, "This sickness will not end in death. No, it is for God's glory so that God's Son may be glorified through it" (11:4). At the tomb, Jesus instructed the stone to be rolled away. Distressed, Martha told Jesus that "by this time there is a bad odor, for he has been there four days" (v. 39). Jesus replied, "Did I not tell you that if you believe, you will see the glory of God?" (v. 40).

Hardness of heart often brings unbelief even in the midst of the miraculous. Even after Jesus had performed so many signs in their presence, they still would not believe in Him. This was to fulfill the word of Isaiah the prophet: "Who has believed our message and to whom has the arm of the LORD been revealed?" (53:1). For this reason they could not believe, because, as Isaiah said elsewhere:

> "He has blinded their eyes
>> and hardened their hearts,
> so they can neither see with their eyes,
>> nor understand with their hearts,
>> nor turn—and I would heal them."

Isaiah said this because he saw Jesus' glory and spoke about him.

(JOHN 12:40–41)

The "arm of the Lord" means the strength of God, the power of God. Do you know why Scripture says that God deafened the people's ears and hardened their hearts? He hardened their hearts after they had hardened their own hearts, because to the degree that we receive a revelation and then say no, to that degree the judgment becomes worse. The greater the light that you have and then reject, the greater the consequences. It was out of mercy that Jesus, knowing they were not going to respond, caused a deafness to come on them. He knew they would not accept Him, and so He removed some of their responsibility by causing their ears to be dulled. This was the mercy of God. Because if they had understood more and still said no, it would have made the judgment on them that much worse.

CONTEND FOR HIS GLORY!

It is so important we understand that *supernatural deeds bring glory to the Father*. We are to be concerned about His glory. We are to contend,[4] saying, "God, I want Your glory!" Jesus died so that God could be glorified. God anointed Jesus so that He could receive glory. The amount of glory God receives is in proportion to how much we believe, how much we will declare, how much we will decree. How much we will, in obedience, having received revelation, move on that revelation so that healings, deliverances, and miracles take place.

As believers we are to do works in the name of Jesus. "And I will do whatever you ask in my name, so that the Father may be glorified in the Son. You may ask me for anything in my name, and I will do it" (John 14:13–14). Why? So that the Son can bring glory to the Father. It is for the Father's glory that God wants to answer our prayers and perform the miraculous so that He, the Father, will receive glory. Anything less than that means we are robbing God of His glory.

Many of you have heard, "Touch not the glory of God." In other words, we are not to boast in the flesh because the glory belongs to Him. One of the ways you can touch the glory of God is not to be a people of faith. That actually amounts to stealing from

His glory. When believers do the works in the name of the Father or in the name of Jesus, the Father receives glory. We can also touch His glory by taking credit for the miracles. Or, even if we don't take the credit, if the people are giving you the credit and you don't redirect the focus to God, the glory has been touched. The following testimony by Mark Endres, who was my first traveling assistant beginning in January 1995, is an incident in which touching the glory unintentionally became an issue. It is also, however, an illustration of an act of obedience related to revelation. When DeAnne and I pastored in St. Louis, Mark and his wife, Tammy, were on our leadership team and we were good friends. Today Mark and Tammy have a powerful ministry of inner healing. I consider their website the number-one site for inner healing resources.

When Dr. Randy Clark asked if I would be interested in providing an example of an act of obedience leading to a physical healing, I must confess that I wasn't very interested. The reason for my hesitancy came from a pastoral and trainer paradigm mindset worldview. My concern was and is that often when telling of wonderful breakthroughs and miraculous moments that occur when praying for the sick, unfortunately, disciples in the church mistakenly turn these moments into a spiritual law rather than just a principle to be aware of or an equipping tool to remember when praying for others. So I felt no unction to provide an example. That is, until this morning.

My daily quiet time in the New Testament was focused on Luke chapter 1. As I read the following words, I felt an encouragement from the Lord that I should tell of one example that I had been thinking about. The words that the Lord highlighted as I read Luke were:

> Many have undertaken to draw up an account of the things that have been fulfilled among us, just as they were handed down to us by *those who from the first were eyewitnesses* and servants of the word. With this in mind, since *I myself have carefully investigated everything from the beginning,* I too decided to write an orderly account for you. . . . so that you may know the certainty of the things you have been taught. [vv. 1–4, emphasis mine]

I think the primary reason the Lord highlighted these verses to encourage me was because the story that I am about to share is an example that occurred at *the beginning* of the time in which Dr. Randy Clark and I traveled together, ministering to others. During the first two weeks of January 1995, the following events transpired.

I was on a flight to Melbourne, Florida, with my pastor and dear friend Randy Clark. One year and ten days earlier, he and four members of our church in St. Louis had been asked to come and minister in Toronto, Canada. Graciously and wonderfully this small church near an airport runway was sovereignly visited by the love and power of God. Four scheduled days of meetings ultimately became twelve years of sustained revival in Canada that impacted millions.

Before our Florida trip, Randy said, "Mark, I will know that this revival is something God wants to continue to impart if I see it happen again somewhere else besides Toronto." He explained that the pastors in the Melbourne area were from various denominational and ministerial backgrounds—Baptist, Presbyterian, Vineyard, Independent Charismatic, and others. Some of these pastors had been meeting for six years to pray together and encourage unity. Randy said he felt that God wanted to honor this type of unity, and He [God] wanted to come because He was pleased by it. My response literally bolted from my mouth. "Randy," I said, "I'm a young man and I have never seen what I would call a *real move of God*—I want to see one!"

Well, let me just say that God heard my cry and did exceedingly abundantly above all I could have asked or thought or imagined!

The word was getting out that there was a move of God happening in the area of Melbourne, Florida. Soon nearby towns and cities were getting the news by word of mouth and radio interviews. As a result, Randy and I were invited to come to Vero Beach, Florida, to minister and serve at a Sunday morning church service. During that church service, as Randy spoke, I had a very specific word of knowledge regarding a young girl. I had a mental picture of a girl with brown hair and was impressed in my mind that she was around eight to ten years old. In this mental picture, the girl was wearing a dress with a floral pattern of blue and pink colors and a hairband made of the same material tied in her hair. The impression went on in my thinking this girl had a speech impediment and the Lord wanted me to blow into her mouth three times and she would be healed.

My reaction was one of terror. I was terrified and yet at peace internally at the same time. I don't know how that can be, but that's how I was feeling. This was the first time I had ever been led or impressed by the Lord to do a specific form of prayer and act of obedience when praying for a physical healing! Randy graciously asked me to share this word of knowledge in front of those who had gathered for the church service. I said, "I have an impression that there is a young girl age eight to ten with brown hair who is wearing a floral pattern dress of blue and pink colors. This girl also has a hairband made of the same material that is tied in her hair. I think this girl may have a speech impediment and I would like to pray for her." Because I had not seen this girl or any other girl during the service, or before, that fit this description, it helped me to know that this impression was probably from the Lord.

A woman stated that this young girl was in the children's ministry area and not in the main service, and that she was going to bring her and her mother to me. When the mother and child walked up to me, I saw that this little brown-haired girl was as cute as a button and dressed exactly as I had seen in the impression. It was a beautiful dress and the hairband was tied in her hair just as I had seen it in my mind. And although I was greatly encouraged when first seeing her and in awe of God knowing her and her circumstances so intimately, I now realized I had to pray for her in the way I had seen in the impression.

I began by introducing myself to her mother, speaking at a volume that her daughter would not hear. "Ms. Jones," I said, "as I pray for your daughter's speech, I want you to know that I felt the Lord has asked me to blow in her mouth three times as I pray. I've never done this before, and I know this is very unusual. Therefore, I would like to ask your permission as her mother if I may do this." She immediately said, "Yes." Next, I turned to the little girl and, without really thinking, found myself asking her the following two questions:

Q: Can you say my name?
A: Maaawwwaakkk (her attempt at saying Mark)
Q: Who loves you?
A: Eeeeassseusssss (her attempt at saying Jesus)

I told her that her answers were correct and I felt Jesus wanted me to pray for her because He had a gift to give her. She nodded her head, giving me a yes. I then asked her to close her eyes and hold out her hands as if she was going to get a gift from Jesus. As soon as I asked her to do that, not only did she close her eyes and extend her hands in front of her with palms up to receive a gift, but to my surprise she also opened her mouth wide. This was incredibly significant and miraculous for me because I had no idea how I would be able to blow three times into her mouth, and frankly, I did not want to ask her to open her mouth. The impression I had received was that I was to blow *into* her open mouth—not just blow on her mouth. So, when she naturally opened her mouth without any prompting, I knew the Lord was with her in a special way.

I prayed: "In the name of Jesus, I bless your speech to become whole and clear." Then I briefly blew three small puffs of air into her mouth. After a moment, I asked her the same two questions I had asked earlier.

Q: Can you say my name?

A: Mark

Q: Who loves you?

A: Jesus

Mom grabbed her immediately and started crying and smiling at the same time. The person who had brought the mother and daughter to me also joined in. I slipped away breathing a silent prayer of thanksgiving to my King and to my Lord and Savior!

There are several things I pray you will take away from this story and process in your heart. First, I want you to know that as wonderful and miraculous and encouraging as this story is, you should not simply start a school of praying for people by blowing into their mouths unless the Lord specifically directs you to do that and you are certain it is the Lord! Of the thousands of people I have prayed for, I have only had the Lord direct me to take a specific course of action or act of obedience on five occasions. When I pray for the sick, I do not wait for specific words of knowledge before I will pray. I ask the Lord to provide words of knowledge as needed, to encourage both those who will be receiving prayer and myself.

Second, when you experience this type of specific leading from the Lord, I encourage you to take the risk in a kind and humble manner. Do not make it the rule of your prayer life, but do obey these moments. Third, when you pray for others, have another person with you whom you trust. This is a great way to ensure that someone else observes that you are being kind and humble and gentle as you obey the leading and apply the act of obedience. In this way we can continue to be teachable and learn when these impressions are from the Lord, or when we may be trying to produce fruit in our own strength, or are actually mistaken.

Finally, if you have never attended one of Dr. Randy Clark's seminars on how to pray for the sick and receive words of knowledge, you must sign up and go as soon as possible! The more you are equipped, the more you will pray. The more you pray for others, the more you will see others healed![5]

ELEVEN

THE FULL MESSAGE OF
THE KINGDOM

THE SON OF GOD APPEARED TO DESTROY THE work of the devil. We see this when Jesus heals the man born blind. "Neither this man nor his parents sinned," said Jesus, "but this happened so that the works of God might be displayed in him" (John 9:3). Jesus' high priestly prayer in John 17:10 says, "All I have is yours, and all you have is mine. And glory has come to me through them." Who is the "them" in that verse? Is it referring to His disciples? Jesus said that glory was already coming to Him through the disciples because they believed His report. They had already found out that even the demons were subject to Him, in His name. This was before Pentecost. Pentecost hadn't even happened yet and Jesus was already receiving glory from the disciples because they had healed the sick and cast out demons.

Jesus said, "I have given them the glory that you gave me, that they may be one as we are one" (John 17:22). He was saying essentially, "Father, You gave Me glory, and I have given that same glory to them, the disciples." This was delegated authority; it was power associated with authority. Again, remember that this was before Pentecost. Jesus said this before He actually began the church. And He said, "I am going to send you what my Father has promised; but stay in the city until you have been clothed with power from on high" (Luke 24:49). And then at Pentecost the glory came. The wind and the fire and the miracles came, and people believed and were converted.

When Peter healed the crippled beggar at the gate called Beautiful and the man went through the temple, walking and jumping and praising God, the people were astounded. And Peter told them, "Fellow Israelites, why does this surprise you? Why do you stare at us as if by our own power or godliness we had made this man walk? The God of Abraham, Isaac and Jacob, the God of our fathers, has glorified his servant Jesus" (Acts 3:12–13).

Much of the church has not understood this message, this reve-lation of what it means to glorify God. I don't say this in judgment but with sadness. But I believe it is a sadness that is going to end soon. I believe it will end when His name is glorified here in North America as it is being glorified right now in Latin America and in Asia and in Africa. I am contending for this. And when Jesus said He has given the glory to us that His Father gave to Him, He was not just talking about giving the saints this glory. Jesus was talking about this glory being given to all who will believe in Him through the Word.

> "I have given them the glory that you gave me, that they may be
> one as we are one—I in them and you in me—so that they may
> be brought to complete unity. Then the world will know that
> you sent me and have loved them even as you have loved me.

"Father, I want those you have given me to be with me where I am, and to see my glory, the glory you have given me because you loved me before the creation of the world." (John 17:22–24)

Let me paraphrase these verses:

"I have communicated to all those who believe, or shall believe in Me, the glorious privilege of becoming sons of God that, being all adopted children of the same Father, they may abide in peace, love, and joy in unity." For this reason it's said in Hebrews 2:11, "[Christ] is not ashamed to call them brothers and sisters."

Jesus was saying that since we have been made one with the triune God through His (Jesus') blood, in this unity believers can experience the glory of God as He shares it with us through the miraculous.

THE KINGDOM OF HEAVEN MESSAGE

When we let the Scriptures speak for themselves, we see that we are to have this power to work miracles. When the apostle Paul said, "Christ in you, the hope of glory," he was talking about empowerment for miracles. It's about the message of the kingdom. That was Jesus' central message. The message of Jesus was never to be truncated to mean only forgiveness of sins. The message of forgiveness of sins was a part of the message of the kingdom. The other part of the message is that the kingdom of heaven is at hand! Therefore, think differently about life because this power of another realm is available to you, the believers in Christ! You have authority. Change your way of thinking. Repent! We have to start thinking that all things are possible, that nothing is impossible. It is in that moment that the glory comes, and creative miracles take place in our midst. And the only thing that keeps them from happening right now is our lack of expectation of it, not believing it because we haven't heard it. It is for that very reason that I have filled this book, and many of my other books, with testimonies.

Someone once asked me, "Have you ever seen a limb grow out?" I said that I had not, but that I know it is true. I have never seen it personally, but it is happening. I have read about it. It happened at Azusa Street. A leg grew out and an arm grew out in the middle of this great outpouring of the Pentecostal movement.[1] My question is, How in the world did this get hidden, this news about the great power to heal at Azusa Street and the birth of the Pentecostal movement? I don't understand it. I was raised Baptist so I had an excuse. I don't mean that negatively. I mean that I had never heard of these things, and so it was not really expected. But for all of you who are Pentecostal and come from these Pentecostal denominations, what happened? Why don't you know?

I was in Mozambique ministering with Heidi Baker and her team when God grew pupils in the eyes of a little girl who had been born blind. She was eight months old and brought to Dr. Tom Jones, who prayed for her. When she wasn't healed the mother brought her to me for prayer. I prayed for her for quite some time. The mother then took her to some of Heidi's students, who continued to pray. Finally, the mother brought her daughter to Dr. Heidi Baker, who began to pray for her, holding her so that she faced her mother. Heidi had an impression to take water and wash the child's eyes out, which she obeyed. As her mother called her name, the little girl opened her eyes to reveal big beautiful brown pupils in both eyes that had not been there before. She was able to see her mother for the first time![2] Heidi had acted on a word of knowledge that involved an act of obedience. As a result, healing was released and the place erupted with praise, giving glory to God. I have witnessed uncounted numbers of miracles over the years that give glory to God, which is why I am so passionate to write and teach and share what God is doing on the earth today. I want God to receive the glory, and I want to build faith for the miraculous so that God can continue to receive the glory He deserves.

BUILDING A CULTURE OF FAITH FOR THE MIRACULOUS

Praise God that more than the gift of tongues happened at Pentecost. I thank God that I have prayed in tongues ever since I was nineteen years old, but for me, it's not about praying in tongues. It's about the power to work miracles. This is the heritage of the church; these are our roots. We need to go back and redig those wells of Abraham, those wells that have been stopped up, because this is our heritage. I want a hunger to go from the head to the heart of every believer. I want this message of Christ in you, the hope of glory, to go from a concept to a reality. I want us to expect healings and miracles. I want us, the church, to build a culture of faith for the miraculous. I wrote an entire book on this subject a few years ago titled *The Healing Breakthrough: Creating an Atmosphere of Faith for Healing*. The first half of the book deals with practices and teachings that hinder faith for healing. The second half of the book draws upon fifty years of ministry and sharing what I have learned from John Wimber,

Blaine Cook, and Omar Cabrera, the three men who had the most impact on my understanding of healing. I share the things I learned from these three men regarding healing, and what the Lord has taught me about how to build faith for healing. The story that follows is an example of God creating faith for healing. Fortunately, I was able to discern what God was doing in the meeting and able to follow the leading of the Holy Spirit.

I was in the city of Belem in northeastern Brazil. I was leading a large, international ministry team who had come at their own expense, from many countries, to help pray for the sick. We went to a Foursquare church. This church was packed; there was no room even in the aisles. There were two thousand people in the sanctuary and another five hundred people outside watching video on a large screen. The atmosphere was electric with faith from the moment the team arrived. During the praying for the sick, there were 1,288 reported healings. It was amazing. My adrenaline was so strong from that meeting I had trouble going to sleep that night.

The next night we went to a smaller Foursquare church. When we arrived, we found the opposite atmosphere. Instead of excitement and faith there was a notable lack of both. We had more excitement and faith on the teams (we had split into three teams that night) than there was in the church. When we arrived, about twenty people were in the building. The pastor took the leadership of the team into his office, where we stayed for the entire time of worship. When we came out, the building was about 50 percent full with about five hundred people present. I began the message by sharing what had happened the night before, showing a brief video of the numbers of people waving their hands across their heads as a sign they had received a healing. Then I shared, "My faith tonight is not in your ability to have faith for healing. My faith tonight is in God's ability to do things in this service to create the gift of faith in you to receive healing." I began by explaining what a word of knowledge was, because if the people I am ministering to don't understand the purpose of words of knowledge, they won't build as much faith. Then I shared the following testimony.

"A few months ago my intern, Marcus Dygert, who is with us tonight, and I were in another Quadrangular (Foursquare) church about an hour from here. Marcus gave a word of knowledge. He saw (as a mental picture) a red helmet with a black face shield. The helmet had white scratches across the top from an accident. Marcus said he believed someone there had been in a motorcycle accident and was suffering from that accident. Immediately a woman pastor who was seated on the platform with about fifty other pastors began weeping out loud. She stood to her feet and began to walk to Marcus to receive prayer. But by the time she reached Marcus, the Lord had already healed her of serious pain issues in her body from an accident that happened more than ten years ago.

The church was quiet as they listened to this story. When I finished, I was about to start the sermon, when a door to my right, in the front of the church parallel to the pulpit, opened and in walked a young couple, more than an hour late to the service. The man came in first, and the young woman followed behind him, carrying in her left hand, for all to see, a red helmet with a black face shield. They obviously had just arrived on a motorcycle. Upon seeing this, I said under my breath to God, "You've got to be kidding me!" I knew this was not a coincidence. It was a divine appointment, a providential moment. I asked the woman if she needed healing. She responded she did, so I had her come to the front for prayer so all could see the healing that was about to happen. This divine setup had created in me the gift of faith that the woman would be healed.

When I began to pray for her several health problems and pain, she immediately felt the heat of God on her. As I was praying for her, God gave me another word of knowledge about pain in between her shoulder blades. Several people stood and were healed in a short prayer. And the woman with the red helmet was healed of all her symptoms—all pain left her body. I went back to the pulpit to once again begin the sermon. However, my ankles begin to hurt, so I said, "I believe there are five people here who have pain in your ankle bones, and if you will stand and move your ankles, rocking from right to left, you will be healed without need of any prayer." The five stood and did what I asked, and all of them were healed in front of the crowd. The same thing happened with knees. I said there were seven people with knee problems. Eight stood, and I prayed a prayer for less than one minute and asked them to check their knees. Seven of the eight were healed.

Once again I prepared to begin the sermon when my right leg began to hurt in the shin bone, and then the femur bone began to hurt. I gave these two conditions as a word of knowledge. I intended to just announce what I was feeling, but when I began to give the word it came out like this: "There is someone here who had a motorcycle accident that resulted in a double break with a shin bone and a femur bone being broken, and you have complications from this accident." A man on the last row stood up. I had him walk to the front. As he did, you could notice a limp. One leg was shorter than the other because of the terrible breaks in his leg from the accident. He was healed and able to walk without a limp.

At this point I realized that God had done what I had declared I believed He was going to do—to create faith in the people for healing. At that point, I felt that God had preached the sermon and I didn't need to preach. What God had done through the words of knowledge and healings had changed the atmosphere from doubt to faith, from boredom to excitement. I invited my team to come to the front of the church to give more words of knowledge and then to pray for people. At the end of the night we had 365 testimonies of healings out of the 500 people present. It was so exciting to see God move as He did by first creating faith for healing and then by healing. Once again I was so excited it was difficult to go to sleep that night.

When we step into the fullness of the warfare prayer of Jesus (the Lord's Prayer) and live in the reality of "Thy kingdom come. Thy will be done on earth as it is in heaven," we will see the miraculous, and He will be glorified. This is such a powerful prayer.

Hallowed be God's name! A hallowed name is one that has glory attached to it. Father, glorify Thy name! Let Your kingdom come and Your will be done on earth as it is in heaven. Let heaven come to earth! The kingdom of God is at hand!

Sickness and disease are not a part of His kingdom. They are not God's will.

HAVE WE SOLD OUR BIRTHRIGHT?

Let us, the church, not adhere to doctrine that puts off everything about God's present power for us. We need to stop putting God's power in the past or in the future millennial kingdom. Paul wrote, "Encouraging, comforting and urging you to live lives worthy of God, who calls you into his kingdom and glory" (1 Thess. 2:12). He did not say "who *will* call you" and did not say "who *called* you." He said, "who *calls* you into his kingdom and glory" (emphasis mine). That is a present-tense verb. When I was saved, I was called. When you were saved, you were called into His kingdom and into His glory. Are we walking in that reality in the present tense, or have we sold our birthright for a pot of porridge called religion?

Are we busy serving the "Great I Was" or the "Great I Will Be" or the "Great I Am"? When Moses asked God, "Who shall I say has sent me?" God didn't say, "Tell them 'I Was' sent you, or 'I Will' sent you." God said, "Tell them 'I AM' has sent me to you" (Ex. 3:14). "Jesus Christ is the same yesterday and today and forever" (Heb. 13:8). Now God, through the gospel, wants us to share in the glory of Christ. In 2 Thessalonians 2:14 He is talking about the call, about being saved: "He called you to this through our gospel, that you might share in the glory of our Lord Jesus Christ." We are called to share in that glory! This is a present reality. When you were saved you were called so that you might share in the glory of our Lord Jesus Christ. What a heritage!

The transfiguration was Jesus' glorification, to prepare Him for the suffering that was soon to come. The Mount of Transfiguration prepared Jesus for Mount Calvary. Peter was talking about Jesus' transfiguration in the cloud of glory:

> For we did not follow cleverly devised stories when we told you about the coming of our Lord Jesus Christ in power, but we were eyewitnesses of his majesty. He received honor and glory from God the Father when the voice came to him from the Majestic Glory [the cloud] saying, "This is my Son, whom I love; with him I am well pleased." We ourselves heard this voice that came from heaven when we were with him on the sacred mountain. (2 Peter 1:16–18)

TO LIVE IN THE GOSPEL

We are not called just to experiences of feeling good or getting drunk in the Lord's Spirit. Sometimes He gives us experiences for a particular purpose, to heal us or to prepare us. But it's not about us. It's not about our experiences. It is about receiving the experience to live a life for His glory. "Whoever wants to be my disciple must deny themselves and take up their cross daily and follow me" (Luke 9:23). It is about receiving such power that we might pick up the cross and do those things that God has told us to do that will cause the world to reject us. Sadly, sometimes it causes the church to reject us. Hopefully it will not be that way forever.

The cross was an instrument to connote suffering. The gospel is not a gospel to come and get saved so you don't have to suffer in the Great Tribulation. The gospel is more. To live in the gospel is to experience salvation and the power of God so you can be faithful in the time of suffering. Some people say that they don't need the Holy Spirit, don't need the baptism of the Spirit, don't need to be filled with the Spirit. If you don't want to do anything beyond your own human ability, you probably won't seek the baptism of the Spirit. If you don't want to bring glory to God, if you just want to be a good, moral person and get to heaven, then just His Spirit in you is enough. But if you want to be a believer who brings glory to God, you are going to need the power of the Holy Spirit on you so you might do those things only God can do. And He gets the glory. Sadly some unbelievers have more belief than believers. There are some people who aren't even committed to Christ but believe in His power to do things.

Jesus experienced the manifested glory in His body that Peter was witness to, which was to prepare Him for the glory of the cross.

Glory is not just a feeling; it is not just for healing. It is also for the purpose of preparing us for difficult times of persecution and suffering related to the mission of God. I am not talking here about suffering from disease and sickness. Evangelicals take the passages about suffering and say that it is meant to show a good purpose, that suffering from sickness brings glory. In the Middle Ages, the Catholic Church identified holiness with sickness as a way of being purified and sanctified. And it came right over into the Protestant church during the Reformation. I do not believe this was a biblical perspective.

I am not speaking of suffering from sickness and disease. It is suffering from being faithful to the call of God on your life; it is the persecution that comes and the rejection that comes during this life on earth. It is about the cost of being a disciple. The Spirit of glory and of God rests upon the persecuted.

> But rejoice inasmuch as you participate in the sufferings of Christ, so that you may be overjoyed when his glory is revealed. If you are insulted because of the name of Christ, you are blessed, for the Spirit of glory and of God rests on you. (1 Peter 4:13–14)

A TRUNCATED GOSPEL

Years ago I heard the Bible Answer Man, Hank Hanegraaff, say that Pentecostals today are Gnostics. I believe he says that because he is operating out of misunderstanding. First John addresses the dangerous heresy of Gnosticism that was prevalent in the first two centuries of the church. This early Gnosticism taught that spirit is entirely good and matter is entirely evil. This is Greek thinking, not Hebraic thinking. The Hebrew believes that the flesh is good because God created it. That is why we are going to get resurrected bodies. Our spirits are not just going to be spirits out there by themselves. Our spirits will be given glorified bodies. But because Gnostics believed flesh was bad, they didn't believe in healing. Why would God want to heal your body when all He cares about is your spirit? That's how we ended up with a gospel that focused only on souls being saved and not also on healing of bodies. And that is a truncated gospel.

Paul said, "Therefore I want you to know that no one who is speaking by the Spirit of God says, 'Jesus be cursed'" (1 Cor. 12:3). John said that if anyone says Jesus didn't come in the flesh, he is of the Antichrist. The true gospel is that God is not only concerned about my life when I get to heaven; God is concerned about my life right now. God is concerned about all aspects of my life. The Hebrew way of thinking is that I don't *have* a soul; I *am* a living soul. And God created my body and called it good. So when we have a gospel that is only focused on our souls being saved and not concerned about our bodies, not concerned about healing, not concerned about poverty, then that is a truncated gospel, a Gnostic gospel. It is not the full gospel.

CHRIST IN YOU, THE BASIS FOR THE POSSIBILITY OF EXPERIENCING HIS GLORY!

We are called to live in the fullness of the gospel. Christ in you, the hope of glory! Christ in you, the hope of miracles! Christ in you, the hope of power! How can we not have expectation for mighty things to happen through us when He is in us and His Spirit is on us? Believe that He is in you! Believe that He is bubbling up in you, that it is Christ in you! Believe that when you begin to get those impressions, He is in you; He is near you—as close as your breath. Let us take our belief beyond those doctrines that have hindered us: an overemphasis on sovereignty, an overemphasis on holiness, and even an overemphasis on faith. Let Him out! Believe! Have faith that Christ in you is the hope of glory!

> "And this is my prayer: that your love may abound more and more in knowledge and depth of insight, so that you may be able to discern what is best and may be pure and blameless for the day of Christ, filled with the fruit of righteousness that comes through Jesus Christ—to the glory and praise of God." (Phil. 1:9–11)

CONCLUSION

MY FIRST DAY OF COLLEGE, GOD IMPRESSED UPON me that the issue of my life would be the Holy Spirit. This has proved to be true to a much greater extent than I could have ever imagined. My Baptist background with its solid foundation in Scripture proved to be an impetus into the fullness of the gospel and helps sustain me during the challenges that continually come my way as I strive to walk as one in whom the fullness of the living Christ dwells. The miraculous of God is not something to distrust. He is known by His fruits, which bring Him glory.

Scripture tells us that all authority was given to Jesus, and we see Him using that authority repeatedly to bring glory to the Father through miracles, signs, and wonders. He instructs us and commissions us to do the same, and even greater works, so that the Father may continue to be glorified on earth.

As we end, I want to share one final story from Mark Endres that focuses our hearts and minds regarding intimacy with God and the supernatural.

We were ministering in Guatemala. Approximately five thousand had gathered in a tent that reminded me of the massive circus tent I had seen as a child. The stage was very large, the tent poles extremely tall and strong. White plastic chairs were everywhere the eye could see, an ocean of chairs. The lighting was so well done that it felt like the middle of the day at 8:00 p.m.

My pastor, Randy Clark, was next to the stage on one side of the tent, and I was on the other side. People had formed a line on both sides from front to back to receive prayer from us. Without any hesitation I can tell you I have never seen more healings take place than I did here. It was beyond wonderful!

However, during one brief moment as I took a sip of water before continuing to pray, I caught a glimpse of just how many people were lined up on both sides wanting individual prayer from Randy or myself. Suddenly, the only way I know how to describe it was I felt the heart of the Holy Spirit grieved that the people were looking to Randy and me more than to God Himself. I immediately excused myself from the person I was about to pray for and went across the tent to Randy. While he was still praying, I whispered in his ear what I was sensing. I could tell this was causing him to have to switch gears. He had just seen a baby that had been born blind receive vision. At this very moment the family's doctor was there with the parents and was testing the baby's eyes and confirming the healing. So it goes without saying that Randy and the family and those near us were in pure unadulterated excitement. This was the environment in which Randy now had to weigh what I had whispered to him. In true humility he immediately got up on the stage, took the microphone, and stated that God wanted us all to ensure that we were looking to Him and not to men. He went on to say that we were all going to return to our chairs and worship for fifteen minutes and that

God was going to break out with spontaneous healing as we worshiped to confirm *who* the source of our healing is from.

As the music began, I remember being on the steps of the stage in a kneeling position just weeping and asking the Holy Spirit not to be grieved. Thanking Him for His guidance and correction and asking Him to know we were sorry and how much we loved Him. During that fifteen minutes, well over five hundred people were healed and spontaneously came forward closer to the stage to worship. The dear pastor of this tent church witnessed a woman directly in front of him experience her back cracking and adjusting as it became totally straight. She had just been healed of spinal scoliosis.

Tantalizing is defined as "having or exhibiting something that provokes or arouses expectation, interest, or desire, especially that which remains unobtainable or beyond one's reach."

Transforming is defined as "to change in form, appearance, and/or structure; metamorphose; to change in condition, nature, or character; convert; to change into another substance; transmute."

I shared the previous story to illustrate that while witnessing and experiencing miracles, healings, signs, and wonders can encourage and strengthen our faith, they in and of themselves have no ability to be the foundation of changing our lives. They are divine, but they are not discipleship. They are wonderful, but they are not our walk. They are tantalizing, but they are not to be confused with our call to transform (Rom. 12:1-2). We are to be led by the Spirit of God, not the good gifts of God.[1]

I have seen thousands of Christians activated in gifts of healing, words of knowledge, prophecy, and other gifts of the Spirit, some by simply receiving the knowledge of how to recognize the various ways God communicates with us and other times through powerful encounters with the Holy Spirit. In all this, we must be careful to keep our hearts fixed on the Giver and not the gifts.

While preaching in Lystra, Paul and Barnabas encountered a man who was lame from birth. Paul, receiving discernment from the Holy Spirit that the man had faith to be healed, commanded him to stand to his feet. At Paul's words, the man jumped to his feet and walked. The crowd that had gathered to hear them preach began to honor Paul and Barnabas as gods when they saw the miracle. When they realized what the people were doing, Paul and Barnabas, tearing their clothes, refused to receive honor. Instead, they preached the gospel (Acts 14:8–18).

God will back up the preaching of His Word with miracles, signs, and wonders today just as He has done throughout the history of the church. Yet, we must be ever mindful to "seek first the kingdom of God and his righteousness, and all these things will be added to you" (Matt. 6:33 ESV). After Jesus fed the five thousand, He realized that the people were about to "come and take him by force to make him king," and so "Jesus withdrew again to the mountain by himself" (John 6:15 ESV). Jesus had no desire for the adulation of the crowds. His heart was always fixed on His Father and God's kingdom and His righteousness.

It is my great desire that all see and understand what God is doing in the world today. I pray that the testimonies in this book and the teaching from Scripture will contribute to your understanding of who God is so you, too, may live as one who sees His will done on the earth today as it is in heaven.

ACKNOWLEDGMENTS

I WANT TO ACKNOWLEDGE MY INDEBTEDNESS TO Susan Thompson, who helped me with the manuscript before it ever reached Janene MacIvor, the editor for Emanate Books. The skillful editing of both of you makes this book a better read. Thank you, Susan, for editing this work and for the many other books of mine on which you served as my editor. Your keen insight and editing through multiple renditions have relieved many of the burdens and stresses that come with taking a book from start to finish. I take full credit, however, for any shortcomings in this book. I also want to thank Timothy Paulson, vice president and publisher for Nelson Books, for allowing me to write on this subject. Thank you for saying yes to my desire for the subject of this book.

NOTES

INTRODUCTION

1. For more information on the Global School of Supernatural Ministry, visit https://gssmusa.com/.
2. I have written about the evidence of the miraculous in Scripture in other books: *The Essential Guide to the Power of the Holy Spirit*; *There Is More*; *Power to Heal*; and *Authority to Heal*. For more resources, see Jon Ruthven, *On the Cessation of the Charismata: The Protestant Polemic on Postbiblical Miracles* (Tulsa, OK: Word & Spirit Press, 2011); and Jon Ruthven, *What's Wrong with Protestant Theology? Tradition vs. Biblical Emphasis* (Tulsa, OK: Word & Spirit Press, 2013). *What's Wrong with Protestant Theology?* discusses the importance of bringing back biblical discipleship, which includes healing and deliverance, not just Bible study. See also Gary S. Greig and Kevin N. Springer, eds., *The Kingdom and the Power: Are Healing and the Spiritual Gifts Used by Jesus and the Early Church Meant for the Church Today?* (Ventura, CA: Regal Books, 1993), 321–43; Gary S. Greig, "The Purpose of Signs and Wonders in the New Testament: What Terms for Miraculous Power Denote and Their Relationship to the Gospel," in Greig and Springer, *Kingdom and the Power*, 133–74; Selby Vernon McCasland noted that the phrase "signs and wonders" in the New Testament largely denotes "ordinary deeds of healing performed by faith." Selby Vernon McCasland, "Signs and Wonders," *Journal of Biblical Literature* 76, no. 2 (June 1957): 151.

3. For evidence of the miraculous in church history, see Ramsay MacMullen, *Christianizing the Roman Empire AD 100–400* (New Haven, CT: Yale University Press, 1984), chapters 3–4. MacMullen emphasizes that the primary reason for the conversion of the Europeans from the Greco-Roman gods to Christianity was the gospel's power to deliver from demons and to heal sickness and disease. He also points out that the last god whose temples were consecrated as churches was Asclepius, the Greco-Roman god of healing. In William DeArteaga, *Forging a Renewed Hebraic and Pauline Christianity* (Tulsa, OK: Word & Spirit Press, forthcoming), DeArteaga adds to MacMullen by pointing out how important healing was to the American church in the final quarter of the nineteenth century and the first part of the twentieth century. See also David Harrell Jr., *All Things Are Possible* (Bloomington, IN: Indiana University Press, 1975). Harrell presents a scholarly portrait of the interest in healing at the mid-twentieth-century. While I was in South Africa, a taxi driver shared that he had left the Pentecostal denomination to join the Zionist movement, a cult in South Africa. When asked what motivated him, he said, "I was healed through the Zionist church, so my whole family and I joined it." This is consistent with the emphasis of MacMullen. See also Henry I. Lederle, *Theology with Spirit: The Future of the Pentecostal-Charismatic Movements in the 21st Century* (Tulsa, OK: Word & Spirit, 2010).

4. For evidence of the miraculous from the mission field, see Randy Clark, ed., *Supernatural Missions: The Impact of the Supernatural on World Missions* (Mechanicsburg, PA: Global Awakening, 2012); Craig Keener, *Miracles: The Credibility of the New Testament Accounts* (Grand Rapids, MI: Baker Academic, 2011); James A. Kelhoffer, *Miracle and Mission: The Authentication of Missionaries and Their Message in the Longer Ending of Mark* (Tübingen: Mohr Sieback, 2000), especially chapter 5; Arthur Tappon Pierson, *The Miracles of Missions: Modern Marvels in the History of Missionary Enterprise, 2nd ser.* (New York: Funk & Wagnalls, 1895); Kim-Kwong Chan,

"Interview: The Miracles After Missions," *Christian History*, no. 52, 1996, https://christianhistoryinstitute.org/magazine/article /interview-miracles-after-missions.

5. However, to think that this revelation is always rational or cognitive in origin is to limit God and His sovereignty. An example of this type of revelation can be found in Daniel 10:4–10. In this experience there is both rational information and the experience of power, trembling, loss of strength, i.e., physical manifestations.

6. Randy Clark, "A Study of the Effects of Christian Prayer on Pain or Mobility Restrictions from Surgery Involving Implanted Materials" (DMin diss., United Theological Seminary, 2013). "Measurement" 182–85; "Analysis of Data" 200–11; "Outcome" 225, 227. Randy Clark, *Eyewitness to Miracles: Watching the Gospel Come to Life* (Nashville: Thomas Nelson, 2018), 184.

7. Jon Ruthven, *On the Cessation of the Charismata: The Protestant Polemic on Postbiblical Miracles* (Tulsa, OK: Word & Spirit Press, 2011), 185–86.

CHAPTER 1: TWENTY-FIRST-CENTURY DISCIPLESHIP AND THE SUPERNATURAL

1. The following scriptures connect either the proclamation or living out the gospel's connection to the power of the Holy Spirit: 1 Cor. 12:8–11; 2 Cor. 4:7, 10:3–4; Eph. 1:18–20, 3:7, 16–21; 1 Thess. 1:4–5; 2 Thess. 1:11; 2 Tim. 3:1–5; Heb. 6:4–6.

2. Randy Clark, *Supernatural Missions: The Impact of the Supernatural on World Missions* (Mechanicsburg, PA: Global Awakening, 2012).

3. Matthew 10:7–8 covers the commissioning of the Twelve; Luke 10:1, 8–9, 17 covers the commissioning of the seventy-two and their report upon their return; Matthew 28:18–20 covers the Great Commission that applies to all believers and should be understood in light of the commissioning of the Twelve and the seventy-two in relation to "teaching them to obey everything I have commanded you."

4. Ramsay MacMullen, *Christianizing the Roman Empire AD 100–400* (New Haven, CT: Yale University Press, 1984), chapters 3–4.

5. For more on Leif's work, visit https://globalmissionawareness.com.

6. For more on Heidi's work, visit http://irisglobal.org.

7. For more on Robby's work, visit https://robbydawkins.com.

8. Matthew 9:37; 25:35–40.

CHAPTER 2: SIGNS, WONDERS, AND MIRACLES IN JESUS' MINISTRY

1. John Wimber, *Power Healing* (San Francisco, CA: Harper and Row, 1987), 245–46.

CHAPTER 3: INTIMACY AND THE MINISTRY OF HEALING

1. C. Austin Miles, "I Come to the Garden Alone," 1913, public domain.

CHAPTER 4: INTIMACY AND FRUITFULNESS

1. Luke 1:37: ὅτι οὐκ ἀδυνατήσει παρὰ τοῦ θεοῦ πᾶν ῥῆμα. "That not (to be impossible) from/by the God all/every word (rhema)." This could literally be translated, "Every rhema-word (freshly spoken) from or by God will not be impossible." The implication is that the word from God contains the power to fulfill itself when understood as a way God works, causing the gift of faith to rise in the heart of the one who hears the word from the Lord. The 1984 NIV translates this verse as, "For nothing is impossible with God." The 2011 NIV translates the verse as "For no word from God will ever fail."

2. Col. 1:29; Luke 4:18; Eph. 3:10 ESV; Matt. 16:18; Mark 3:27.

CHAPTER 5: UNDERSTANDING OBEDIENCE

1. Luke 6:19–20, 8:42–54; Matthew 9:20–22, 14:34–46.

2. This term "Jews" used by John refers to the Jewish leaders who were hostile to Jesus, and it is not a reference to the Jewish people as a whole.

CHAPTER 6: THE RELATIONSHIP OF OBEDIENCE TO HEALING AND MIRACLES

1. Randy Clark, ed., *Supernatural Missions: the Impact of the Supernatural on World Missions* (Mechanicsburg, PA: Global Awakening, 2012), 378–79.

Chapter 7: Christ in You, the Hope of Glory

1. MacMullen, *Christianizing the Roman Empire*, chapters 3–4.
2. Romans 8:11; 1 Peter 1:3–4; Ephesians 1:14. Colossians 1:27: "To them God has chosen to make known among the Gentiles the glorious riches of this mystery, which is Christ in you, the hope of glory."
3. Colossians 1:29: "To this end I strenuously contend with all the energy Christ so powerfully works in me."
4. Ruthven, *On the Cessation*, 22.
5. Morton Kelsey has written about this influence in his book *Healing and Christianity*. However, when writing my thesis I was informed by a leading Roman Catholic theologian that Kelsey had misunderstood Aquinas, and that Aquinas was very open to the supernatural and the gifts of the Holy Spirit. I believe Dr. Mary Healey is correct and Dr. Kelsey has misunderstood Aquinas. However, I do believe there was an eventual influence from rationalism associated with Aristotelian philosophy that created less room for the supernatural in the church. In this way it is true that Luther and Calvin, along with the other major reformers, did not challenge the sixteenth-century understanding of the faith, which was much less open to the supernatural than the earlier periods of the church.
6. Emphasis mine. Also note how much this sounds like the prayer of a "Word of Faith" minister. The faith cure movement and the Word of Faith movement both based their faith for healing on the promises of God's Word and would remind God of these promises. Luther was doing the same thing.
7. Henry Worsley, *The Life of Martin Luther*, vol. 2 (London: Bell and Daldy, 1856), 326–27.
8. Worsley, *Life of Martin Luther*, 286–88. Emphasis mine.
9. Theodore J. Tappert, *Luther: Letters of Spiritual Counsel* (1960; repr., Vancouver, BC: Regent College Publishing, 2003), 48–49.
10. Theodore Jungkunz, "Charismatic Renewal," *Concordia Theological Monthly* 42, no. 1 (1971): 5–23.

11. Thomas Boys, *The Suppressed Evidence: Or, Proofs of the Miraculous Faith and Experience of the Church of Jesus Christ in All Ages* (1960; repr., 1832), 192–204.

12. Ruthven, *On the Cessation,* 22.

13. Ruthven, 22–24.

14. Ruthven wrote a section of the book—Part Three: A New Biblical Understanding of the Baptism of the Spirit by Dr. Jon Ruthven, (Destiny Image, 2017), 131–60.

15. Ruthven, 25.

16. Ruthven, 26. Bosworth, *Christ the Healer,* 101.

CHAPTER 8: THE GLORY AND THE CROSS

1. Karl Marx, *A Contribution to the Critique of Hegel's Philosophy of Right,* vol. 3. Marx's reference to religion is a reference to Christianity, for that was the dominant religion of the continent and the basis for his evaluation. This was before Pentecostalism had begun and much of it was either Roman Catholic, Lutheran, or Calvinist.

2. Leon Morris, *The Cross in the New Testament* (1965; repr., Grand Rapids, MI: Wm. B. Eerdmans, 1999). See especially the conclusion. 404–19.

3. Morris, *Cross in the New Testament,* 404–19.

4. Gustaf Aulen, *Christus Victor: An Historical Study of the Three Main Types of the Idea of Atonement,* trans. H. G. Herbert (New York: MacMillan, 1969).

5. Matthew 16:18.

6. Matthew 13:33.

7. John Wimber, *Power Healing,* (San Francisco: Harper and Row, 1987), 157. Wimber's understanding on the now-and-not-yet aspect of the kingdom of God was influenced by George Eldon Ladd, who wrote *The Kingdom of God* (Carlisle, UK: Paternoster Press, 1959), 13–51, esp.; Derek Morphew, *Breakthrough: Discovering the Kingdom* (Capetown, South Africa: Struik Christian Books, 1991), 155–56.

8. John 2:11, 11:40; Rom. 1:4, 6:4; 1 Cor. 15:42–43; 2 Cor. 3:18, 4:7.

9. A more extreme view of sovereignty is that of the Reformed camp, which believes all that happens is included in the sovereignty of God and nothing happens that is not due to His will or not permitted by His will. In connection to healing, the knowledge would cause one to believe God caused or allowed the illness to come upon them; and if so, why would we think it is now His will to heal us? Another consequence would be if we prayed and the person wasn't healed, it was because it wasn't God's sovereign will to heal them. Everything is due to predestination in one sense—God is in control of all things.

10. Eddie Hyatt, *2000 Years of Charismatic Christianity: A 21st Century Look at Church History from a Pentecostal/Charismatic Perspective,* revised and updated (Dallas: Hyatt International Ministries, 1998), 26, 212–14. Other causes of weakness in the Church: institutionalization of the bishops (23–30); lower morality among Christians than in earlier times (18); et. al. for all these causes.

11. Raniero Cantalamessa, "The Catholic Charismatic Renewal: A Current of Grace for the Whole Church," Charis, https://www .charis.international/en/the-catholic-charismatic-renewal-a-current-of-grace-for-the-whole-church/.

CHAPTER 9: PERSECUTION, TRIBULATION, AND GLORY

1. 1 Peter 1:6–7, 4:12–16, 5:4, 9–10.

2. He wrote under a pseudonym that was a Jewish name: Juan Josefat Ben-Ezra. His book was on prophecy, called *The Coming of the Messiah in Majesty and Glory.* Edward Irving, a Presbyterian proto-pentecostal learned Spanish so he could translate the book into English. Edward influenced John Darby, the Father of Dispensationalism. Edward's book would be put on the list to be destroyed by the pope. Lucanza was influenced by another Jesuit, Franscisco Ribera, who wrote in the late sixteenth century about the Antichrist being a Jew. The development of futurist views has been influenced by this book.

3. For more information, visit https://www.irisglobal.org.

4. Timothy Opeyemi Omole, *Divine Healing Among the Pentecostal Churches in the 21st Century, with Reference to the Christ Apostolic Church in Southwestern Nigeria,* https://www.academia.edu/39156728/Divine_Healing_among_the_Pentecostal _Churches_in_the_21st_century_with_reference_to_Christ _Apostolic_Church_in_south_western_Nigeria, 4–6. Moses Oludele Idowu, *"An Instrument of Revival: The Story of Joseph Ayo Babalola, the First Apostle and General Evangelist of the Christ Apostolic Church,"* a paper presented to an international religious conference on the origins of Christ Apostolic Church, the first Pentecostal churches in Nigeria and Ghana, jointly organized by the Centre for World Christianity (CWC) of the New York Theological Seminary (NYTS), Joseph Ayo Babalola University (JABA), Ikeji Arakeji, Osun State, Nigeria, and the Institute for Diasporan and Afrjcan Culture (TIDAC), Joseph Ayo Babalola University, August 6–8, Lagos, Nigeria (Divine Artillery Publications, 2012), in the section "Meeting with the Nigerian Faith Taberrnacle."

5. *A Select Library of Nicene and Post-Nicene Fathers of the Christian Church,* 2nd ser., vol. 13 (New York: Christian Literature Co., 1898), 84–85, quoted in "Pope Gregory the Great, Letters, 598–601," http://bcs.bedfordstmartins.com/WebPub/history /mckayunderstanding1e/0312668872/Primary_Documents /World_History/WC29-Pope%20Gregory%20the%20Great%20 Letters_ed-ka.pdf. (The quote begins on the third page of this document, with the beginning of the first full paragraph.)

6. John 15:8.

7. Hebrews 4:16.

8. Ephesians 2:6.

9. Philippians 2:12.

10. Corrie Ten Boom, *Tramp for the Lord* (New York: Jove Books, 1978), 105.

11. Available through Amazon as a Kindle edition (https://www .amazon.com/Ministry-Training-Manual-Randy-Clark-ebook /dp/B006O4SN0A) and through Global's bookstore in

paperback or PDF in English, Spanish, and Portuguese (https://globalawakeningstore.com/product/ministry-team-training-manual/).

CHAPTER 10: HOW GOD REVEALS HIS GLORY

1. Ephesians 2:8: "For it is by grace you have been saved, through *faith*—and this is not from yourselves, it is the gift of God" (emphasis mine).
2. Galatians 5:22: "But the fruit of the Spirit is love, joy, peace, forbearance, kindness, goodness, *faithfulness*" (emphasis mine).
3. Mel Tari, *Like a Mighty Wind*. (Green Forest, AR: New Leaf Press, 1971).
4. Colossians 1:29: "To this end I strenuously *contend* with all the energy Christ so powerfully works in me," emphasis added. Contend means "to strive, fight, struggle" (Accordance Bible Software).
5. Mark Endres, *Real Revival: From Roots to Fruits* (St. Louis, MO: HOJM, 2016), 10; Mark and Tammy Endres, *When Heaven Seems Silent: How to Wait on God's Promises Through Pain, Disappointment and Doubt* (Lake Mary, FL: Charisma House, 2014), 10–11. (This long excerpt is a direct quote from an email Mark sent to me asking for a testimony of an event he remembered while traveling with me.)

CHAPTER 11: THE FULL MESSAGE OF THE KINGDOM

1. Tommy Welchel and Michelle Griffith, *True Stories of the Miracles of Azusa St. and Beyond: Relive One of the Greatest Outpourings in History That Is Breaking Loose Once Again* (Shippensburg, PA: Destiny Image, 2013).
2. Clark, *Supernatural Missions*, 366.

CONCLUSION

1. Endres, *Real Revival*, 45–47. (This is a direct quote from Mark, sent to me in response to reaching out to former travel companions and interns or associates.)

ABOUT THE AUTHOR

RANDY CLARK is best known for helping to spark the movement of God now affectionately labeled "the Toronto Blessing." In the years since, his influence has grown as an international speaker. He continues, with great tenacity, to demonstrate the Lord's power to heal the sick. Randy received his master of divinity from the Southern Baptist Theological Seminary and his doctor of ministry and doctor of divinity from United Theological Seminary (Dayton, Ohio). He has written more than forty books, and his message is simple: "God wants to use you." The most important aspect of his calling to ministry is the way God uses him for impartation.

John Wimber heard God speak audibly the first two times he met Randy, God telling John that Randy would one day go around the world laying his hands on pastors and leaders for the impartation and activation of the gifts of the Holy Spirit. In January 1994, in the early days of the outpouring of the Spirit in Toronto, John called Randy and told him that what God had shown him about Randy a decade earlier was beginning now. It has continued ever since. Randy has the unique ability to minister to many denominations and apostolic networks. These have included Roman Catholics, Messianic Jews, Methodists, Reformed, Lutheran, many Pentecostal and Charismatic congregations, and the largest Baptist churches in

Argentina, Brazil, and South Africa. He has also taken several thousand people with him on international ministry teams. Bill Johnson says the fastest way to increase in the supernatural is to accompany Randy on an international trip. Randy has traveled to more than fifty-four countries, including 116 trips to Brazil through 2019, and he continues to travel extensively to see that God's mandate on his life is fulfilled.

Randy and his wife, DeAnne, reside in Mechanicsburg, Pennsylvania. They have four adult children, all married, and eight grandchildren.

For more information about Randy Clark, his ministry, and his resource materials. visit:

www.globalawakening.com

To invite Dr. Randy Clark to minister, contact his personal assistant:

Vicki@globalawakening.com

For more information about Global Awakening Theological Seminary, visit:

https://Seminary.FamilyofFaith.edu

NOTE FROM AUTHOR

*The Global Awakening College of Ministry and the
Global School of Supernatural Ministry*

I am passionate about education that is practical, biblical, useful, and that increases the fire and anointing of students. I take seriously the commission of Ephesians 4 to equip the saints for the work of ministry. As such, Global Awakening offers opportunities for multiple stages of life and just about any budget, from our eight-week online certification courses to our three-year on-site school of ministry.

Through our Christian Healing Certification Program and the Christian Prophetic Certification Program courses, we have seen several thousand released into healing and prophetic ministry. These online courses are now included in the courses that are offered through our Global Awakening College of Ministry, which has added courses in theology, biblical studies, and leadership. Church planting and church growth courses will be added in the near future. Global Awakening Theological Seminary courses on physical healing, inner healing, and deliverance were likewise built upon those in the certification programs previously mentioned.

Presently, a master of arts degree is offered in biblical studies, along with a master of arts in evangelism, and in pastoral ministries. The master of divinity degree is offered in two focuses; as an MDiv in Bible and an MDiv in ministry. Global Awakening Theological Seminary is the graduate program of Family of Faith Christian University. For more information visit:

https://seminary.familyoffaith.edu/about/

It is our desire and prayer to offer doctoral programs in the future.

For more information about the Global Awakening College of Ministry and the Global School of Supernatural Ministry go to:

https://globalawakening.com/education